Public
Relations
in Practice

PR IN PRACTICE SERIES

Public Relations in Practice

Edited by Anne Gregory

Second Edition

the Institute *of* Public Relations

KOGAN PAGE

London and Sterling, VA

First published in Great Britain and the United States in 1996
Reprinted 1998
Second edition 2004

120 Pentonville Road
London N1 9JN
United Kingdom
www.kogan-page.co.uk

22883 Quicksilver Drive
Sterling VA 20166–2012
USA

British Library Cataloguing in Publication Data

A CIP record for this book is available from the British Library.

ISBN 0 7494 3381 7

Library of Congress Cataloging-in-Publication Data

Public relations in practice / edited by Anne Gregory.--2nd ed.
    p. cm.
Includes bibliographical references and index.
    ISBN 0-7494-3381-7
    1. Public relations. 2. Public relations--Great Britain. I. Gregory,
Anne, 1953-
HD59.P795 2003
659.2--dc22

                        2003022065

Typeset by Jean Cussons Typesetting, Diss, Norfolk
Printed and bound in Great Britain by Clays Ltd, St Ives plc

Contents

About the authors

Robert Blood specializes in risk issues, the psychology of public opinion, and activist groups. He has worked on a wide range of issues from animals in medical research, through chemicals in the environment, to the ethics of medical regulation. Most recently he has been closely involved in interpreting the GM issue.

Robert speaks and writes regularly on the nature of public opinion and the psychology of communications. For several years he ran Mind Link, the IPR's psychology interest group. Trained as a physicist at the University of Durham, he is a former board director of Fleishman-Hillard UK Ltd and the Quentin Bell Organisation plc. He now lives in Freiburg, Germany.

Terrence Collis, Director of Group Corporate Communications, Lloyds TSB. A distracted chemist at Durham University, Terrence was lured into public relations with stories of long lunches and foreign trips. After a very short period in consultancy in 1975 (he was sacked) he took to in-house communications and worked his way to the centre of power, becoming director of public affairs for Vickers plc in 1988. A second spell in consultancy was more successful as managing director of Lowe Bell Financial for five years, before returning to corporate communications as director at NatWest and subsequently his current role at Lloyds TSB.

He is still hoping for those long lunches and foreign trips to materialize.

Phil Crossley BA Hons, MIPR, Head of External Relations North East – Royal Mail Group. After obtaining a first class honours degree in Graphic Design Phil followed a career in advertising and publicity before joining Yorkshire Water where he carried out several roles including Customer Communications Manager during the drought of 1995 and Customer Services Manager. Phil then joined The Post Office (Royal Mail Group) as Director of Communications in the North East Division in 1998, subsequently becoming Head of External Relations.

Phil is a member of the Institute of Public Relations and a previous Chairman of the IPR Yorkshire and Lincolnshire Regional Committee.

Beryl Evans, FIPR, has extensive experience in directing and managing communications in both the public and not-for-profit sectors, and has received national awards for change management programmes, campaigns and market research.

She began her career with the Greater London Council, moving to Surrey County Council and then the Association of County Councils. She has been an internal communications consultant and recently headed the British Red Cross public relations team. She is currently Chief Executive of the National Gardens Scheme, a charitable trust that raises money for nursing and other charities by opening gardens of quality, character and interest to the public.

Fiona Fountain is principal partner of Fiona Fountain Associates, a small, established agency specializing in the not-for-profit sector. She has worked in the field of communications and fundraising for over 25 years for commercial, statutory and voluntary organizations and prior to establishing FFA, she was Chief Executive of a national charity.

A member of the Institute of Fundraising and the Institute of Public Relations she has served on a number of committees for both bodies. In 1990 she co-founded Fifth Estate (the IPR group for the voluntary sector) and chaired the group for a number of years. Currently a council member of the IPR she is a former judge for the IPR Excellence Awards for the 'not-for-profit' category.

Anne Gregory is Director of the Centre for Public Relations at Leeds Metropolitan University and the UK's only full-time Professor of Public Relations. Originally a journalist, Anne spent 10 years in public relations practice at senior levels both in-house and in consultancy before moving on to an academic career. Anne is President-Elect of the Institute of Public Relations (IPR) and was created a Fellow in 1999. She initiated and edits the Institute's *Public Relations in Practice* series of books and is managing editor of the *Journal of Communications Management*.

Anne is actively involved in PR practice as a consultant and is a non-executive director of South West Yorkshire Mental Health NHS Trust with special responsibility for finance and communication.

Ardi Kolah FIPR, FCIM, Chartered Marketer, has over 15 years' marketing, public relations and sponsorship experience within the public and private sectors. He is a Director of the Institute of Public Relations and The European Sponsorship Consultants Association. He holds a postgraduate Masters degree in law from King's College and University College, London and is the author of *Essential Law for Marketers*, published by Butterworth-Heinemann. He writes a regular column for the leading marketing communications portal, Brand Republic (www.brandrepublic.com)

Tony Langham is Chief Executive of Lansons Communications, the specialist financial services consultancy he co-founded with Clare Parsons in 1989. Since then Lansons has grown one person and one client at a time to become the largest in financial services in the UK – and the 27th largest agency overall in the 2002 *PRWeek* League Tables.

Lansons has pioneered 'best practice' in UK consultancy since its formation. Twenty-two people (out of 60 in total) own significant stakes in the company and the company's 'creating tomorrow's leaders' development programme was recognized by the PRCA in its 2002 awards. Lansons won the 'Outstanding achievement by a Public Relations Consultancy' award from the IPR in 2002, and was *PR Week*'s 'Consultancy of the year' in 1995.

In the 1980s Tony worked in market research, strategic planning and public relations for MORI, then Dewe Rogerson.

Martin Le Jeune read history at University College London and worked in marketing before joining the civil service (Cabinet Office) in 1986. Among other posts, he advised on senior-level training policy in the civil service, before becoming private secretary to successive Ministers for the Arts and Civil Service between 1989 and 1992.

He was seconded to National Westminster Bank for two years in 1993 as head of public policy, and on returning to the civil service, became the assistant secretary of the Committee on Standards in Public Life ('the Nolan Committee'). Martin drafted considerable sections of the first three Nolan Committee reports.

Martin joined Fishburn Hedges in 1998 and is a board director and head of the company's corporate responsibility practice. He has worked on public affairs, corporate reputation management and corporate responsibility issues.

Martin was a founder member and former chair of the standards committee at the London Borough of Lambeth, and a director of the Association of Professional Political Consultants (APPC). He is a trustee of the whistleblowers' charity Public Concern at Work and he has written extensively on political, ethical and corporate responsibility issues.

Richard Moore has been at the forefront of sponsorship and PR for over 14 years and has developed strategic programmes and implementation for a wide number of award-winning sponsorship campaigns.

Richard formed Capitalize Ltd in March 1996, aiming to invigorate the sponsorship industry and develop creative campaigns with a marketing backbone for corporate clients. Capitalize has developed a quality portfolio of major clients including Schroders, Bacardi-Martini, Carlsberg-Tetley, Hi-Tec and Britannic Asset Management, and has been responsible for high profile campaigns through sport, music, broadcast, the arts and new media.

Richard is a director of ESCA, the European Sponsorship Consultancies Association, and has been credited with helping to build sponsorship as a crucial element of the marketing mix.

Prior to embarking upon a career in sponsorship Richard was a member of the British sailing team.

Pamela Mounter is a corporate communication consultant and lecturer. She has more than 20 years' experience of internal and external communication management in Europe, Africa and the

Caucasus with the oil industry, agribusiness and the non-government sector. A childhood in Africa and postings to Brussels and Baku developed her understanding of the importance of culture and its influence on communication. She is a member of the Institute of Public Relations, where she is leading a project to define a truly global model for public relations, and is on the advisory board for Thames Valley University's MSc in Communication.

Alan Smith, BA (Hons), FIPR, is Director, Public Relations for one of the UK's largest construction services organizations, HBG Construction Ltd, part of the £5.4 billion turnover European construction company Koninklijke BAM Groep nv (Royal BAM Group). A graduate of the University of Leeds, he is a Fellow of the Institute of Public Relations and is Chairman of CAPSIG, the Construction and Property Special Interest Group of the IPR. Alan is also on the Executive Committee of IBP, the International Building Press group, is author of several papers on community relations and co-author of two books concerning corporate communications and marketing in the construction industry.

Carl Welham, MIPR, is head of corporate communications and marketing at Sheffield City Council. The role has a unique combination of the full suite of communications, marketing and promotional vehicles alongside the Council's customer service interface. Carl has worked for three previous councils in his 10-year public sector PR career. Prior to entering the world of PR, Carl worked as a social action radio producer with BBC local radio and had his own theatre company.

Lionel Zetter is a Fellow of the Institute of Public Relations and a Member of the National Union of Journalists. He is Chairman of the IPR's Government Affairs Group. He has worked for several MPs, and has been actively engaged in Conservative politics for many years, chairing two local associations, working at Conservative Central Office and being on the Approved Candidates List. He is a former Associate Director of the Media Information Group, and Company Secretary of PR+CI Ltd. He is now Managing Director of Parliamentary Monitoring Services Ltd, a political research, publishing, polling and campaigning company.

Preface

The first edition of this book was written in 1996. It certainly reads now as if it were written in the last century, but at its time it was absolutely leading edge!

That is the world of public relations practice. Fast moving and always changing. What it is all about, however, remains the same. Public relations is about managing the relationship between an organization (or individual) and its various stakeholder groups. It does that through communication and the aim is to achieve mutually beneficial results, one of which may be an enhanced reputation. So while the discipline remains essentially the same, the tools that we and our stakeholders use have evolved and changed the nature of our business.

In 1996 the Internet was in its infancy, mobile phones were owned by a fraction of the population and laptop computers were dreamed of by most. Now all these things are commonplace and practice reflects this change. Furthermore, business was riding high and the Internet bubble, Enron and Worldcom were all to come.

As a result, stakeholder groups such as NGOs and issues such as corporate social responsibility did not feature at all in the first edition of this book, but have now placed themselves firmly on the agenda. NGOs and pressure groups are major players in organizational life and they, perhaps more than any other group, have used the new technologies to get their voices heard. Indeed, they have shifted the balance of power in their favour so much that many of these groups that were once ignored as full of unimportant, powerless cranks now have to be taken seriously by society at large.

So, the content of this book has changed to match the changes in practice. The first chapter is entirely new and looks at the public relations industry as a whole. It takes a rain-check on where the industry is now: the progress it has made and the questions that are still being posed. It then looks at the wider issues affecting the industry and at those factors that it needs to address to ensure its future progress.

The chapters on marketing communications, financial public relations, business-to-business, internal communication, sponsorship, community relations and not-for-profit public relations have all been re-written to reflect the substantial developments in those areas: indeed many are unrecognizable from the earlier version!

The chapter on government and local government relations has been split to reflect the massive growth in the public sector in particular.

There are entirely new chapters on corporate social responsibility, NGOs and public relations in the service sector, which recognize the emergence of these areas of practice.

The book has been written by authors who come from both in-house and consultancy and without exception they are all at the forefront of their field of expertise. I would like to express my thanks to them for sharing their knowledge with the wider public relations community.

1

Public relations in practice: the 21st-century landscape

Anne Gregory

Dynamic, fast-moving, always developing, at the heart of the action. These are the words and phrases that truly reflect the nature of public relations practice in the 21st century. Indeed, it would be absolutely accurate to say that never before have the opportunities for public relations been so great. More and more organizations are recognizing the value of communication, whether they are countries, royal families, fast-moving consumer goods producers or environmental activists. As a result the industry is burgeoning and pro-fessional communicators are seeing their influence grow as organizations acknowledge their importance.

This chapter aims to set contemporary public relations into context. It will do that in three ways. First, it will give a brief status report, looking at where the industry stands in terms of growth and development. Second, it will look at the environment in which practice is undertaken so that some of the main opportunities and challenges that confront the industry, both now and in the future, can be identified. Third, it will examine the industry itself and pick out some key issues that are emerging and that need careful consideration. These issues can be grouped under three main headings: 'big picture', people and practice.

First then, a look at the industry now: at its progress and at some of the questions still being asked about it.

AN INDUSTRY IN THE ASCENDANCY

According to the UK Institute of Public Relations,[1] the industry is growing at about 17 per cent per year, all the FTSE 100 companies have public relations departments and public relations is one of the top three career choices for graduates. An increasing number of communicators are full board members within companies and, in the public sector, the developing stakeholder engagement agenda has provided extensive opportunities for public relations professionals.

Globally, the industry is expanding and is currently worth about £3 billion. Not only are global organizations and public relations consultancies basing their communication professionals around the world, but also indigenous public relations industries are now responding to the communication challenges of their own environment. The formation of the Global Alliance of Public Relations Institutes[2] in 2002 recognizes not only the growth of global communication and of institutes around the world, but the need for professional bodies to both promote and regulate the profession.

Public relations professionals are being employed in every walk of life. From government to the smallest voluntary group, public relations assistance is regarded as essential. Public relations brings to the public notice issues of great importance such as social justice, the environment, government policy, global trade and religions. It provides a voice to those who might have remained unheard and opens up to public debate matters of life-changing significance.

In its noblest manifestation it can help bring together those of fundamentally opposed positions and look for ways to reconcile differences and resolve conflict. Less obviously, it can also work as a non-vocal agent of change in organizations, subtly changing cultures by setting and moulding the communication context and helping to interpret change to organizational stakeholders.

Although still used extensively in a marketing communication context, largely product or people promotion (which still accounts for 70 per cent of public relations activity[3]), public relations' role in managing relationships with a whole range of key stakeholders such as the financial community, government, local community, suppliers, employees and pressure groups, is increasingly recognized. Indeed the emergence of the stakeholder[4] approach by organizations has provided public relations with a golden opportunity to consolidate its central position within the senior management of organizations.

Furthermore, the growing requirement for companies to report both formally and informally on their non-financial performance as part of the drive to good governance generally,[5] means that corporate social responsibility in the round is moving up the agenda and this is natural territory for public relations. At last, alongside the financial figures presented in Annual Reports and Accounts and given equal prominence and importance is an assessment of the value of the intangible assets of organizations. This material is often generated by the public relations department and provides the basis for a comprehensive evaluation of a company's true worth. These are rigorous inputs by public relations and are helping reinforce the position of the discipline as being one of substance.

A healthy sign of the industry's vibrancy is the growth in public relations courses around the world. Full-time undergraduate and graduate courses are providing a pool of knowledgeable entrants to the industry and part-time courses for working practitioners are helping to improve standards and ratchet-up the performance and qualification platform of the industry. These courses demonstrate that public relations is beginning to fulfil one of the key requirements for gaining recognition as a fully fledged profession ie, a solid, articulated knowledge-base. Public relations is building its own 'body of knowledge', undertakes research and is developing specific curricula for its courses. This commitment to education and training shows a level of maturity in the industry and mirrors the development of other professions such as law, medicine and accountancy.

So in many ways public relations has not only 'arrived', it is thriving and making headway in ways only dreamed of just five years ago.

An industry facing significant questions

Despite the undoubted progress that has been made, there are still significant questions being asked about public relations.

In the political arena there have been a number of unfortunate scandals. The infamous 'Jo Moore incident' where the special adviser to the then UK Transport secretary Stephen Byers advised colleagues to bury any bad news on 11 September 2001, did nothing to enhance the reputation of those involved in political communications. Accusations of 'spin' are rife in this area and are immensely damaging not only because they tarnish the reputation of public relations, but because people become cynical about the political process and disengage from politics – very dangerous in a democracy. Furthermore, there are huge questions in the public mind about the ethics of lobbying. The popular view, whether accurate or not, is that those rich and powerful enough to employ professional lobbyists are in some way over-influencing the legitimate decision-making process.

Public relations in the field of business also comes in for criticism. Communicators are often seen to be justifying the unjustifiable, such as large increases in pay for executives whose businesses are failing, or business decisions that are clearly purely profit-driven but disguised as something else. The problem here is that communicators themselves are associated with these business decisions and their integrity questioned.

A great deal of public relations effort and creativity goes into marketing products of little consequence or promoting arrogant or greedy celebrities. Is public relations thereby encouraging the trivial, voyeuristic or purile and what effect does this have on the reputation of the industry?

Some key questions about public relations remain. Is it a real profession? Is it about propaganda and spin when it gets down to it? What are the ethics of the industry? Is it about serving the interests of the rich and powerful or is it about serving society as a whole? How, on the one hand can public relations be involved in the trivial, but on the other want to be recognized in the boardroom? Are there clients and causes that should be refused? In other words, public relations still lacks a level of legitimacy.[6] All these are serious questions for the industry, which require working through and cannot be dodged.

Having provided an overview of the industry, it is important to look at some of the broader, contextual factors that will impact on it and that will need to be taken into account as practice develops in the 21st century.

THE BROADER LANDSCAPE

There are dozens of developments in the external environment that affect the practice of public relations. This section will focus briefly on a few of the most important, but the list should not be regarded as at all definitive. Chris Genasi[7] and Michael Morley[8] have provided good overviews in their books.

Globalization

It is a truism to say that we now live in a global village. But are the implications of this really understood by public relations practitioners? Clearly those who work for global organizations will understand the need to communicate in a way that is appropriate across timelines, cultures, religions, languages and communication delivery systems. It's more than that. It's being globally aware. It is recognizing that even if you don't work across countries, what you do in your locality may have a global impact. So if your local restaurant in Islington uses prawns bought from a local fishmonger who imports from India, you might be helping a developing nation's trading position, but are you aware of the employment conditions of the prawn fishermen and what are your responsibilities for this?

It is being aware that what you trumpet on your Web site to the UK market may be offensive to someone from another culture who accesses that Web site thousands of miles away.

Information and information technology

This, of course, is closely linked to globalization. Again, the ability to send or access information instantly and across any time or geographical barriers brings both opportunities and threats to the public relations practitioner. Crises can escalate unseen, activists can organize quickly and inaccurate information can be transmitted worldwide, all at a few clicks on the mouse.

Alternatively, definitive information about a crisis can be provided, corporate information sent and dialogue conducted over continents in real time and 24/7 in as many different media formats as you please. All this brings a great deal of pressure on practitioners who need to provide constant cover, be vigilant and adroit at spotting opportunities.

There is also the issue of technology disparity. While the developed world goes on apace, able to conduct worldwide communication via the mobile phone thanks to 3G technology, there are whole nations that are struggling to provide even the most basic technology to their citizens or government departments. So it is vital that professional communicators do not become too seduced by evolving technologies and then find they are unable to contact whole stakeholder groups who do not have access to these technologies.

Interdependence

This factor is linked to the preceding two. Our world is becoming massively interdependent. This is true of our personal lives: we depend on others for our food, clothes, transport and housing. It is also true of organizational life: we depend on suppliers, customers, the local community, employees and so on. The age of self-contained self-sufficiency is over. Again this provides enormous opportunities for the public relations professional because at all stages up and down the dependency value chain there are points of contact that are potential sources of conflict and/or cooperation. Communication and understanding are critical to the smooth running of this value chain. The fact that these dependencies now spread across the globe adds a level of complexity that is part of everyday life. Managing these relationships in a mutually beneficial way is an invaluable contribution that public relations can make to any organization.

Pluralism

This is a difficult one and is contradictory in some ways. By pluralism is meant the merging of values and ideals. We live in a society that is generally more tolerant of people who believe in different things and who act outside 'the norm'. Thus great strides have been made in people trying to understand different cultures and religions and there is more acceptance of alternative lifestyles such as homosexuality. All these are laudable advances in society, many would say. However, this is accompanied in many Western countries by a decline in religious belief and a questioning of traditional authority figures, and this has led to a feeling of insecurity for many people. They also feel they cannot assert a particular position for fear of offending someone.

Thus communication, particularly on sensitive issues such as the environment or cultural matters, is especially difficult. No matter how careful you are, you're likely to offend someone! Furthermore, few public relations practitioners have any formal education or training in subjects such as ethical decision-making frameworks, psychology or conflict avoidance and resolution. So they are thrown back on their own intuition for guidance. As a result, their communication advice and behaviour can be inconsistent and based on the apparent demands of the particular situation they face at any one time.

Consumerism and individualism

Ironically this is the reverse of pluralism! People in the 21st century are very aware of their rights and their ability to assert their individuality. There have never been so many consumer groups, pressure groups, special interest societies and clubs of all kinds. Partly as a reaction to the lack of certainty created by a pluralistic society, people are seeking to associate with others of like mind on issues that concern them as an individual. This is rather different from the more community-based mindset of yesteryear when whole communities, often geographically linked, faced issues together, such as localized unemployment and social problems.

Today's professional communicator has to deal with much more assertive consumers whose rights are increasingly enshrined in law and who do not necessarily recognize their balancing obligations. Furthermore, pressure groups, often made up of people emphasizing their individuality, are an increasing factor of organizational life and a challenge both for good and ill for the communicator who may be responsible for establishing relationships with them.

The media

The media are clearly changing. The downsizing of the media

industry, the burgeoning number of channels, the 24/7 nature of the business, along with the changes in media ownership, have altered it massively.[9] Journalists are under increasing pressure and are becoming more dependent on public relations sources to supply copy.[10] This is partly because they do not have the time to undertake original research or to check alternative sources, but also because in some areas such as political and celebrity public relations, the public relations practitioners themselves are powerful gatekeepers who can deny access to popular and sales-guaranteeing individuals. The move of journalism from investigation to infotainment and the near obsession with celebrity has meant that there is less space for serious discussion of topics of real importance to society.

Two things come from this. One is the danger that public relations itself becomes more focused on the trivial because that is where the easy media 'hits' can be had. Second, the relationship between public relations and journalism becomes unhealthily close. While the gratuitous PR-bashing indulged in by many in the media is both dishonest and unnecessary, it is only right that the media are genuinely free to make critical judgements, to uphold the public interest. This is threatened if they become over-dependent on public relations sources that are often unashamed in their bias, although readers remain blissfully unaware.

ISSUES FACING THE INDUSTRY

Recognizing the overall context in which PR operates, it is now appropriate to look at some of the key issues facing the industry itself under the three headings mentioned earlier ie, 'big picture,' people and practice.

Big picture issues

The previous section outlined factors in society as a whole that are affecting virtually every aspect of personal and working life. On top of these there are some overarching issues facing the PR industry that also merit consideration.

The first is to do with the overall direction of travel for the PR industry. The status report at the beginning of this chapter gave an indication of where the industry is at this point in its development.

It now faces a choice: does it want to become a real profession or does it want to remain a craft industry?

Jacquie L'Etang[11] in her analysis of the industry, identified three areas that continue to be problematic if public relations wants to become a formally recognized profession. First, the lack of a cognitive base, that is, research-based, expert knowledge that underpins the industry. The position is slowly improving as the theoretical aspects of the subject are gradually being established,[12] but there is a way to go yet before anything comparable to the accountancy, legal or marketing base is available. The second area is that PR has no clear jurisdiction ie, it does not control its own occupational boundaries like other professions such as medicine. Public relations is encroached upon by all kinds of other functions including management consultancy, HR and marketing who claim the territory as their own. The third area is a lack of social legitimacy ie, the social role and value of public relations is not recognized, neither is there an acknowledgement of the standards that constitute ethical practice.

Add to these three concerns a requirement that entrance to a profession should be by examination only, that there should be specified client protocols and a fiduciary relationship with clients, and it can be seen that public relations has some way to travel yet, but is on track. Initiatives like the Public Relations Consultants' Association Management Standards and the scoping of public relations done by XPRL.org[13] and academics all help.

There are of course many people who think that public relations should not become a profession and that it is and should always be a skills-based craft where technical capabilities like good writing, design and an ability to work with the media are what are really important. So the internal debate within the industry goes on: does public relations want to move on to be a profession, with all that that entails, or to remain an unregulated, technical craft?

Allied to this is how the practice is developing in the field. On the one hand there is an apparently insatiable demand for the technical skills of public relations people. As implied earlier, the media have a voracious appetite for pre-prepared stories or copy. Furthermore, clients want to see their name and products in the newspaper. Moves towards payment by results[14] and an increasing amount of project work, while maybe not bad in themselves, are forcing consultancies in particular to focus on short-term results, often media coverage or short-term sales that demand a tactical approach.

A consultancy is only as good as its last short-term project. On the other hand, the demand for strategic board-level advice is also increasing as organizations require their public relations experts (usually in-house based) to look after long-term reputational agendas and to develop sustainable, brand-building campaigns.

So we can see a divergence within the industry: one direction beginning to become more and more tactical, the other being more and more strategic. Put this together with the 'Do we become a profession?' discussion and we can see a division being forced on the industry almost by default. There are clear parallels in other professions, for example accounting technicians and professions allied to medicine undertake highly skilled and valued inputs, but nevertheless they are not recognized as the 'top flight' professionals, ie, the fully qualified accountants and doctors who have undertaken a rigorous, prescribed education and who reap the rewards for that in terms of pay, professional prestige and social recognition.

Certainly if public relations practitioners are to claim a seat at board level they will have to get beyond special pleading for a set of communications skills that can in reality be learnt fairly quickly by anyone. They will have to demonstrate that they are business managers with the normal knowledge-base of any other senior business manager and that, in addition, they can contribute a well-grounded understanding of the business, the business environment, stakeholders and how relationships with them are best managed through communication.

The final 'big-picture' issue facing the public relations industry is that of communication convergence. It is an absolute fact that the communication disciplines are converging and technology is forcing the pace. The arbitrary distinctions that currently differentiate between, for example, public relations and marketing, are being recognized as just that. Marketing is just another name for managing the relationships with customers and customers are just another, although vitally important, stakeholder group. Public relations practitioners would be foolish not to grasp the opportunity to rightfully claim that they are the natural stakeholder managers. However, this is not a responsibility to be taken lightly. It is one thing to claim the territory and another to demonstrate that you have the knowledge and skills to undertake the task well.

People issues

There are some increasingly pressing concerns facing the industry to do with the employment and development of the workforce. A major factor here is the increasing number of women coming into the industry. In this public relations is not alone. The law, medicine and accountancy face the same issue. However, there are some things that flow from that.

The stereotypical employment pattern of women is that they come into an industry, work hard, make a success up to middle management and then take a career break to have children. They then return and either decide to stay at essentially the same level so that they can maintain a work/life balance, or move on and upwards.

The signs are that in public relations, many capable young women are not returning to the industry after a career break. This is partly explained by the fact that the industry has notoriously long and unsociable working hours and it tends to be demand-driven (media requirements, client demands). With children, this working pattern is not easily sustainable, so many women leave at this stage or return to do a 'technician' job because it is more manageable. It is precisely at this point that they could have made the transition to becoming senior managers and/or strategists, so there is a capability gap that is likely to grow wider as the proportion of women increases and the mainly female output from the relatively new public relations undergraduate courses moves upwards in the industry. This could provide more opportunities for the smaller proportion of men to advance more quickly than they might have!

Then there is the issue of ongoing training. While it is true to say that the industry is getting better at investing in training – there are many more training courses and training oportunities[15] – it is still relatively poor at planned ongoing training and there is no compulsory continuing professional development. Thus poaching is rife among the larger organizations and there are no consistent standards among small consultancies, sole practitioners or small in-house departments.

There is also a question about the overall composition of the public relations workforce. It is predominantly middle-class, white and female. If public relations is about managing relationships with all stakeholder groups, this is best done by the industry being more reflective of all stakeholding groups in society. The industry can only benefit from recruiting from ethnic minorities and from the full range of social classes who bring their in-depth knowledge and open-up access to wider stakeholder groupings.

Finally in this section, while it is true that a great deal has been done to address the intake quality of the industry through undergraduate courses and professional body membership examinations, there is still little training and development at the most senior levels. The industry has still to see major inroads at postgraduate level in the business schools. Although there are a growing number of Masters level courses in PR, there are very few MBA courses that have substantial amounts of public relations in them and relatively few PhD students in the subject.

To round off this chapter, a number of key day-to-day practice issues have been identified that warrant specific discussion.

ISSUES FACING PRACTICE

The practice of public relations has developed amazingly over the last few years. Some of the issues identified here represent recurrent themes, some are relatively new. All of them will need concentrated, combined effort if they are to be resolved properly. Unfortunately, most of them lay practitioners open to be picked off as individuals. The role of the professional bodies in providing a lead cannot be over-emphasized, both to demonstrate value-added for the membership community, but also to drive the industry forward for the benefits of members and clients alike.

Evaluation

A great deal of progress has been made in this area, with initiatives like the Research and Evaluation Toolkit published by the UK Institute of Public Relations setting the pace. What has been clearly established are the notions of input (what the practitioner produces), outputs (how that 'product' is used), outtake (what messages are abstracted from the 'products') and outcome (the actual results either at a thinking, attitudinal or behavioural level). It has also been accepted that measurable objectives based on solid research must be an integral part of programme planning and that evaluation entails measuring whether those objectives have been met.

However, most of this work is posited on the idea that the organization sets out to achieve an objective in a very purposeful way. While this may be true, public relations is also about listening to stakeholders, and organizations changing as a result of their concerns. There is nothing substantive in the evaluation domain on this. Neither is there much on measuring the quality of relationships that are established, and this is critically important.

Disaggregation, value for money and intellectual property

There is a real push now to measure the value of public relations. Terms that are used are 'return on investment', 'impact on the bottom-line', and 'the specific contribution of public relations'. This is difficult because public relations is often one element in a raft of communication activities including advertising, word of mouth, sales literature and so on. Some useful work is being done in this area, but more is required if a financial value (among others) is to be put on the discipline. On the other hand, there is no doubt that public relations can be seriously undervalued.

The public relations industry is in the intellectual services business. It lives on its brains, but it gives its ideas away! The whole business of putting a value on creative aspects of public relations work is in serious need of attention. There is no doubt that some clients 'steal' ideas from the pitching process and there is no doubt that some clients pay minimal amounts for public relations campaigns that generate enormous amounts of business for them. A serious discussion on the value of intellectual property, creativity and payment for (as opposed to by) results is long overdue and the public relations industry has a strong hand to play.

Transparency

This is especially true in the consultancy world. Much more transparency is required on costs and processes. Clients demand to know exactly what they are paying for, who is working on their account and what they are doing. Questions are being asked such as, are there ways of using technology such as XPRL to make processes more cost-effective? What are the management overheads and how can retainers be justified? The involvement of purchasing departments and the use of Service Level Agreements are making consultancies much more accountable.[16] Clients are wise to the fact that it is often cheaper to employ someone in-house to do the standard public relations tasks such as press release writing and house-journal editing and are requiring more value-added services from consultancies. For in-house practitioners similar questions are being asked by senior managers who want to know that they are getting value for money from their public relations departments.

IT and 24/7

We are in a business that never sleeps! The media, crises, financial markets and global communities all function 24/7 and are supported by enabling technologies. The demands on practitioners to run an all-year-round, never-sleeping function are here.

The industry needs to think through how it responds to these ceaseless demands. It requires careful thought about the deployment of staff, IT-enabled information resources, the physical location (or not) of offices and staff, and the kind of services that should be legitmately offered by a modern-day public relations service.

CONCLUSION

So there it is, an overview of the context in which public relations operates. This introductory chapter has outlined:

● where the industry is now;
● the wider context in which the industry operates;
● the specific issues facing the industry itself.

The following chapters will demonstrate how diverse and demanding public relations work is.

Together, this chapter and the ones following show why public relations is one of the most challenging, demanding, exciting and per-sonally rewarding careers there can be. Public relations is at the cutting edge of organizations; at the 'point where issues collide.'[17] It is not for the faint-hearted, but it is infinitely rewarding for those who want to make a difference to themselves, their organizations and to society.

Notes

1. For further details about the PR industry see www.ipr.org.uk.
2. For details about the Global Alliance see www.globalpr.org.
3. Moloney, K (2000) *Rethinking Public Relations*, Routledge, London.
4. Freeman, R E (1984) *Strategic Management: A stakeholder approach*, Pitman, Boston, MA.
5. At the time of going to press the new Companies Bill is likely to require more extensive reporting on a company's environmental, employee and governance matters.
6. L'Etang, J (2002) Public Relations education in Britain, *Journal of Communication Management*, **7** (1) pp 43–53.
7. Genasi, C (2002) *Winning Reputations*, Palgrave, Basingstoke.
8. Morley, M (2002) *How to Manage your Global Reputation*, Palgrave, Basingstoke.
9. See Moloney, K (2000) op cit, for an overview.
10. See Stauber, J C and Rampton, S C (1995) *Toxic Sludge is Good for You*, Monroe, Common Courage Press, for a view on the effect of corporate public relations on the media agenda.
11. L'Etang, J (2002) op cit.
12. Hutton, J G (1999) The Definition, Dimensions and Domain of Public Relations, *PR Review*, **25** (2) pp 199–214.
13. See www.XPRL.org for information on scoping the domains and activities of PR.
14. 'Pay as you go', *PR Week*, 11 October 2002.
15. See IPR website, www.ipr.org.uk for approved training courses.
16. 'The art of pitching', *PR Week*, 11 October 2002.
17. Pearson, R (2000) Beyond ethical relativism in Public Relations, in eds J E Grunig and L Grunig, *Public Relations Research Annual*, Vol 1, pp 67–86.

2

Marketing communications

Ardi Kolah

INTRODUCTION

You've turned the page and arrived at Chapter 2. And the title of the chapter is 'Marketing communications'. Have you made some mistake? The cover of the book says 'Public Relations in Practice', so what has marketing communications got to do with public relations? And what's the relationship between public relations and marketing?

Sometimes it's easier to explain what you don't do. As with all definitions, the lines aren't always clear. Public relations (PR) draws on expertise and experience from many fields and it frequently overlaps with other disciplines, including marketing. On one hand, this is a strength, but it's also a weakness when it comes to providing an absolute definition of what is meant by 'PR' as this is open to subjective interpretation.[1]

The IPR Web site[2] provides the following definition of PR: 'public relations is about reputation – the result of what you do, what you say and what others say about you.' The IPR then continues to explain this further:

Public relations is the discipline which looks after reputation, with the aim of earning understanding and support and influencing opinion and behaviour. It is the planned and sustained effort to establish and maintain goodwill and mutual understanding between an organisation and its publics.

This is very often confused with marketing, which is understandable. To many marketing practitioners and academics, public relations is part of the 'promotions' part of the 4Ps – product, place, price and promotion – that make up a successful marketing campaign. However, a caveat should be added here. Public relations can best play a role in creating a successful campaign when all the other elements of the marketing effort are also present and are integrated with public relations:

Advertising doesn't build brands, publicity does. Advertising can only maintain brands that have been created by publicity. The truth is, advertising cannot start a fire. It can only fan a fire after it has been started. To get something going from nothing, you need the validity that only third-party endorsements can bring. The first stage of any new campaign ought to be public relations.[3]

As long ago as 1989, marketing guru Philip Kotler saw public relations as one of the most cost-effective components of marketing communications:

Marketing practitioners are very likely to increase their appreciation of public relations' potential contribution to marketing the product because they are facing a real decline in the productivity of their other promotional tools.[4]

Today, those words are still relevant. Advertising costs on television, radio and print have continued to increase in real terms. In addition, brand owners and organizations have to cope with the fragmentation of media (as a result of digital channels and the Web) as well as the fragmentation of audiences. As a result, traditional channels of communication are failing to deliver value and return on investment.

Sales promotions and incentives may look attractive, yet there is absolutely no evidence that these mechanisms actually help to drive sales without other communication tools and techniques being employed. Public relations, on the other hand, has continued to deliver value because of its lower costs comparative to other forms of marketing communications as well as efforts to measure both its output and effect. Kotler adds: 'The creative use of news events, publications, social investments, community relations and so on offers companies a way to distinguish themselves and their products from their competitors.'[5]

Who the brand owner and organization is trying to reach will dictate what channels of communication are used as part of the marketing mix. There is a whole variety of options, as can be seen in Figure 2.1.

Figure 2.1 *The marketing communication mix*

WHAT IS MARKETING?

At a basic level, marketing is the presentation of a proposition in the way in which it is most likely to be accepted – irrespective of whether it is the packaging of Pedigree Chum dog food, Tony Blair's 'War on Terrorism', *Who Wants to be a Millionaire* or *The Sun*.

'Marketing' can be defined in various ways. Non-marketers typically think of it as advertising and promotion, but marketers consider that as being too narrow. They see marketing as a whole company or organization activity whereby the goals of the organization are achieved through first achieving the customers' goals. In other words, profits arise from securing customer preference.

An alternative but consistent view is that 'marketing' refers to all activities that generate and harvest an organization's inward cash flow.[6] This description of marketing is concerned with why customers spend money and what would cause them to spend even more and more frequently in ways that are less expensive for the brand owner and organization to service. But this also takes a narrow view, as 'marketing' can have a wider meaning when applied to political parties or individuals, such as the Democratic Party, George W Bush, Victoria Beckham or even Norman Cook aka Fat Boy Slim.

Marketing guru Ted Levitt described marketing as 'getting and keeping customers'. That's right, but marketing is also about:

- The process of planning and executing the conception, pricing, promotion, and distribution of ideas, goods, and services to create exchanges that satisfy individual and organizational objectives.[7]
- A brand owner's business philosophy, which gives priority to satisfying customers' wants and needs as a means to achieving the brand owner's goals. In this sense, marketing as a customer-oriented culture can be applicable to non-profit organizations as well as businesses.
- What the brand owner's marketers do – typically, developing and launching products, packaging, branding, pricing, advertising, promotion and distribution.
- The sourcing and harvesting of inward cash.

The Chartered Institute of Marketing in the UK defines marketing as the management process responsible for identifying, anticipating and satisfying customer requirements profitably. In the context of this description of marketing, public relations is the engine for successful marketing communication.

THE ROLE OF MARKETING IN ORGANIZATIONS

An organization's 'DNA' is made up of several complex parts. For example, the identity of the organization can be defined by examining its mission, vision, values and culture. This identity, which can be summarized as 'how we do things, how we say things and what we believe in', drives the way in which products and services are delivered to various audiences, such as loyal customers, suppliers and even employees.

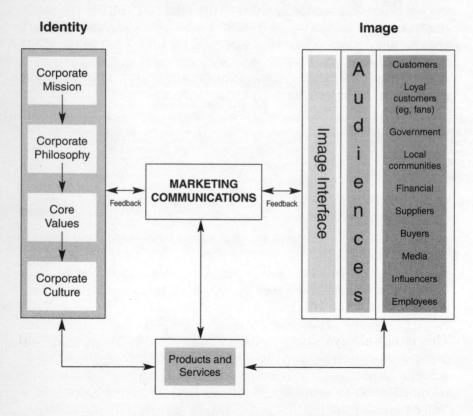

Figure 2.2 *The role of marketing communications*

Marketing communications sits at the heart of this process – that part of a brand owner's or organization's 'DNA' that distils the identity of the organization, managing the image interface with various audiences as well as helping to promote products or services, which in turn forms part of the organization's image interface; see Figure 2.2.

Public relations' contribution

The role of public relations in the marketing mix is simple: it's to communicate key messages to defined target audiences within the marketing chain to influence purchasing behaviour. The same could be said of all marketing communication disciplines: the key difference between public relations and all other forms of marketing communication is the element of external or third-party endorsement, such as positive media comment, a satisfied customer testimonial or independent research carried out by a respected body like the Consumers' Association.[8] This third-party endorsement arguably has more impact on the audiences in terms of its credibility (see Table 2.1).

As a result of gaining credibility through third-party endorsement, public relations can:[9]

- create a market environment;
- increase visibility and/or share of voice;
- inform/educate the consumer;
- influence the trade;
- support a sales force;
- harness influential/opinion formers;
- extend promotions;
- hype advertising;
- exploit sponsorship;
- manage issues;
- contain crises.

This is not always easy to achieve and some brand owners and organizations have attempted to take short cuts in the hope of achieving the same results in less time. For example, 'hybrid public relations' such as 'advertorials' in magazines and newspapers and 'informercials' on TV and the Internet are a half-way house between an advertisement and information/editorial.

Table 2.1 *Channels of marketing communications*

	Public Relations (Internal/External)	Advertising	Sponsorship	Hospitality	Licensing and Merchandising	Direct Marketing	Direct Selling	Sales Promotions and Incentives	New Media
Definition	Public relations is about the management of reputation – the result of what you do, what you say and what others say about you. It is the discipline that builds and maintains reputation, with the aim of earning understanding and influencing opinion and behaviour. It is the planned and sustained effort to establish and maintain goodwill and mutual understanding between an organization and its publics.	Draws attention or describes in favourable terms goods or services or corporate aims and objectives, usually on a paid for basis.	A commercial arrangement where one party (the property) seeks a commercial benefit from another (the sponsor).	Providing a social benefit to a third party (guest) in the context of business.	The exploitation of intellectual property rights (trademarks, copyrights, patents, designs) by licensing the use of these to a third party (licensee) for use across product categories (merchandising).	Sending a targeted message to an individual or selected target group in a precise and focused effort where there is a 'call to action' required from the recipient.	A direct approach from one individual to another, usually in a sales situation.	A device, such as a competition, that is designed to induce or incentivize the purchaser of a product or service to enter in the sales promotion expectation of getting a prize or something of value.	This is the generic term for the Web, Internet, mobile communication, broadband and emerging technologies such as 3G that are new channels of communication.

Table 2.1   continued

	Examples	One-way or two-way communication?	Uses of this channel
	News releases, speeches, events, press kits, seminars, news conferences, annual reports, trade shows, exhibitions, demonstrations, lobbying, internal communication activities, in-house magazines, newsletters.	Two-way	Where you need to communicate with diverse audiences and the media is the most cost-efficient way to do so, which can lead to changes in perception and behaviour of the target audience.
	Press, TV and radio advertising. Banners and pop-up boxes on the Web, advertorials (look like editorial but have been paid for).	One-way	Where you seriously want to impress an audience – the message you want to deliver lends itself to being the centre of a campaign to grab attention and influence behaviour.
	Sponsorship of a football team, an individual pop star's concert or the educational material used in the classroom.	Two-way	Where you want to take the audience with you through 'experiencing' the brand and its relationship with a property that is important to that audience.
	Entertainment offered by a sponsor at a football stadium, race course or art gallery.	Two-way	Where you need to strengthen or reinforce an existing relationship with a target group in a personal way – modern-day customer relationship management.
	Replica football club shirts, branded merchandise of pop stars, T-shirts, baseball caps with logos.	One-way	Where you need to leverage value from intangible assets such as trademarks and allow the audience to 'own' a bit of the magic of the brand, film, movie, pop star, football club, etc.
	Fax mail, e-mail, TV shopping, catalogues, tele-marketing, electronic shopping, voice mail, text messaging.	One-way	Where you need to connect directly with existing or new consumers or wish to change loyalty amongst target groups.
	Sales presentations, product demonstrations, client evenings, incentive programmes, samples, fairs and trade shows.	Two-way	Where face-to-face communication is the only effective way of getting the message across at the point of sale, for example a car showroom.
	Contests, competitions, quizzes, prize draws, coupons, money-off vouchers, sampling, freebies.	One-way	Where you need to breathe new life into an existing campaign or want to create content that can be advertised, promoted, etc as the basis for a new campaign, eg a competition linked to the sale of beef burgers.
	Text messaging, broadcasting, interactive gaming, Sony Playstation, X-box, Nintendo, Sega platforms.	One-way/Two-way	Where you need to reach a youth audience in a credible way.

Table 2.1 *continued*

What it can deliver	Management of reputation, management of the flow of information (internally and externally), consistency of messages, single voice, brand building, targeting of messages in a professional way.	Complete control (subject to law and advertising regulations) over what you want to say and how you say it. Can achieve stand-out from competitors and demonstrate the personality of the brand/ organization. Also is evidence of success and growth (corporate, advertising recruitment advertising). Also 'brand fame'.	Builds a relationship between a brand, a property and fans in a way that goes beyond the confines of advertising.	Relationship building in a non-sales environment.	Extends the brand reach into existing and new audiences and allows the brand experience to be 'owned' as a piece of merchandise, making it a very powerful tool of communication, eg Star Wars merchandise.	Targeting of individuals where additional sales from existing customers is required or where brand loyalty can be displaced in favour of a competitor where price is a key factor in the decision-making process for the customer.	Can influence the customer in a direct way particularly on high-value item purchases where there is a need to ask questions directly of the supplier.	Excitement, interest, publicity for the campaign, cut through against competitor's advertising campaigns.	Another dimension to the brand values, making the brand or organization look 'cool', 'hip', have 'street cred', etc.
What it cannot deliver	No guarantee that the media or audiences won't misinterpret messages delivered. Will need to add	It cannot deliver a two-way dialogue or create a deep level of	On its own, sponsorship is useless unless totally exploited by	It cannot guarantee business or be used as an inducement to enter into	No guarantee of commercial success for the property or the licensee – there is also a risk	Although there may be less wastage (in terms of targeting effort)	It cannot guarantee a successful outcome and may be very costly in	No guarantee of an uplift in sales linked to the sales promotion	Simply using this channel of communication cannot

Table 2.1 *continued*

research to discover whether the messages were received, understood and led to a change in behaviour as a result.	understanding.	other channels of communication including public relations.	a contract (this may be a criminal offence in certain circum-stances).	that it could backfire and lead to negative public relations 'rip off', etc.	compared with, say advertising, there is no guarantee that direct marketing pieces are read (junk mail). Also dependent on the type of technology used (ie sending letters requesting a donation from those already donating money to a charitable cause only damages that organiza-tion's reputation.	time. Not the most efficient way of getting a message across to a large audience.	and incentive (although this myth has been around for years!)	change a boring brand with no relevance to a youth market. There has to be 'real' synergy between the message and the medium.

Table 2.1 *continued*

	Complements all other channels to audience segment/market.	Sponsorship, licensing and merchandising, direct marketing, direct selling, sales promotions and incentives.	Public relations, advertising, hospitality, sales promotions and incentives, new media.	Sponsorship.	Public relations, advertising, sales promotions and incentives.	Advertising, direct selling, new media.	Direct marketing, new media, advertising, sponsorship.	Advertising, public relations, new media.	Public relations, sponsorship, licensing and merchandising.
Other channels that work well with this one.									
Cost-efficient or expensive?	Cost-efficient	Expensive	Cost-efficient	Expensive	Cost-efficient	Cost-efficient	Expensive	Expensive	Cost-efficient

These types of activities are failing to deliver credibility for brand owners and organizations that use them because audiences are becoming more adept, not less, at screening out blatant advertising messages they don't want to receive – no matter how attractively these may be packaged.

For example, text messaging (mobile communication) is favoured by many brand owners and organizations as a platform for reaching a youth audience. No matter how much effort is made to make such communications appear like public relations, they are (mostly) advertising and sales promotions. As a result, these messages are subject to a separate set of laws and regulations – which genuine public relations isn't.[10] This is another advantage of public relations that is often overlooked within the relative strengths and weaknesses of the marketing communications mix.

So while the marketing team creates special price campaigns, discounts, point of sale displays, advertising and direct mail campaigns, public relations can provide support in a different way. As with other marketing tools, public relations can provide a direct channel to audiences, for example through consumer magazines and Web sites.

SELLING PRODUCTS AND SERVICES

Microsoft's Xbox didn't fly off the shelf, audiences didn't queue up overnight to see the latest Harry Potter movie and Badly Drawn Boy didn't pick up the 2000 Mercury Music Award without one vital ingredient – public relations.

It's simply no longer sufficient to create a market-leading product or service. Building a bigger and better mousetrap won't necessarily mean that you'll automatically corner the market for rodent repellent devices.

Brand owners and organizations must go much, much, further. It's now about communicating with audiences in a way that is relevant, meaningful and engaging – which is where public relations comes into its own. Brand owners and organizations are starting to move away from only applying a rationally based approach to marketing communications that focuses on promoting the features and benefits of a product or service and are moving towards an approach that is also concerned with the *behaviour* of those audiences.[11] In short, brand owners and organizations are increasingly exploring ways in which they can influence and change behaviour by listening and talking to their audiences.[12]

In the past, certain brand owners and organizations approached public relations in the manner of 'public announcement relations' – hardly in the spirit of mutual understanding and a genuine attempt to communicate. Over the last 30 years there's been a gradual shift away from this one-dimensional approach to an inclusive one.

The accent here is first to actively listen, consider, engage and then communicate back. For example, Virgin did this when it entered the executive business travel market and took market share from British Airways. The Labour Party did this to win the 1997 General Election and displaced a Conservative Party that had remained in power for 15 years. Most recently Shell did this to rebuild its tarnished reputation in the face of international criticism of its operations in Africa and its environmental track record.[13]

But are these examples of 'PR spin' winning out over substance?

SUBSTANCE OVER STYLE

This is a debate that will probably continue until the end of time! Is effective public relations about substance or style? Is it a bit of both? The Government is often accused of news media manipulation and 'spin'. Whilst this may be over-cynical, it does raise some interesting issues.

The style of communication has an influence on whether the message gets through to the intended audience and whether it's believable. This year, 2003, may well be remembered as a vintage year for 'foot in the mouth' style public relations. The most famous exponent of this technique is Saddam Hussein's former 'spin doctor' Iraqi Information Minister Mohammed Saeed al-Sahhaf. Sahhaf became a familiar face in homes around the world from the start of the Gulf War. His daily 'news' briefings have now become the stuff of folklore. Classic lines included: 'Our initial assessment is that they will all die,' delivered at the beginning of the war and, 'There are no American infidels in Baghdad. Never!', spoken as US troops surrounded the city. Sahhaf disappeared after American forces entered central Baghdad, but not before insisting: 'They are going to surrender or be burned in their tanks.'

Even US President George W Bush admitted that he enjoyed Sahhaf's briefings so much that he used to interrupt some of his meetings just to watch him on TV. 'He's my man, he was great,' he told NBC in a TV interview. 'Somebody accused us of hiring him and putting him there. He was a classic.' Perhaps not classic PR but there's now a Web site dedicated to his 'PR efforts': http://www.welovetheiraqiinformationminister.com.

Later in 2003 it was the turn of the World Health Organization (WHO). The WHO declared the city of Toronto as a no-go area because of the Severe Acute Respiratory Syndrome (SARS) outbreak, which killed more than 200 people and infected almost 4,000 worldwide. On the face of it, the WHO appeared to be acting in the best interests of public health, except that the announcement came as a shock to the Canadian Government and the Prime Minister of Canada who promptly moved his Cabinet to Toronto in the hope that the economy wouldn't become bankrupt. Shortly afterwards, the WHO retracted its unprecedented warning about the risks of visiting Toronto.

Other public relations models include audience feedback (two-way asymmetric) but this has its limitations since the focus is on changing the audience's behaviour alone. The IPR Excellence Awards recognizes campaigns that engage in genuine two-way (symmetric) communication that does not just change public attitudes but also leads to changes within the brand owner or organization itself. A diverse range of entries that achieved this level of public relations performance included a campaign to engage the Scots in an action on world poverty by World Vision; the investigation of missing teenager Milly Dowler by Surrey Police; and the promotion of 'grossology' – a science campaign that appealed directly to kids to visit the Science Museum in London.

Apart from symmetric communication, all these public relations campaigns had one other thing in common – they all used segmentation techniques in order to define their target audience.

SEGMENTATION OF AUDIENCES

Effective public relations as an integral component of successful marketing communications requires a depth of understanding audiences and what motivates them. For example, the financial services industry is extremely complex and a myriad of regulations laid down by the Financial Services Authority casts a complex web over the use of virtually all forms of marketing communications involving pensions, stocks and shares, unit trusts and other types of investments. The idea is to protect consumers and ensure that they understand what kind of products they are buying. It also tries to ensure that people aren't sold inappropriate products. The effective use of public relations allows for more meaning and understanding to be added to the communication effort, unlike, say, a 30-second TV commercial or a poster.

Segmentation of audiences is at the heart of successful public relations and the science of segmentation is becoming more and more sophisticated. Table 2.2 shows an example of segmentation of an audience by the adoption of new technology. The chart represents a major shift in how brand owners are approaching segmentation of audiences and typifies modern public relations practice.

In the past, most brand owners and organizations defined targets in terms of product groups or channels, or sometimes in terms of customer group size. The problem with these approaches to segmentation was the fact that these groupings didn't closely reflect *customer needs* and in fact used the wrong language – which is internally rather than externally focused.

For example, the life insurance market includes customers with very different needs, both rational and emotional. As a result any offering to the market will only ever satisfy some of them and the 80:20 law of effort (80 per cent of profit comes from just 20 per cent of customers) will limit the return on investment. By contrast, today's successful brand owners and organizations with strong marketing strategies define their targets in terms of real segments: groups of people with similar needs who respond similarly to a core proposition.

IMPACT OF PUBLIC RELATIONS ON THE MARKETING EFFORT

IBM's public relations is much more tightly focused as a result of this segmentation model. The use and adoption of technology is critically important to a wide variety of IBM's clients worldwide and traditional segmentation techniques based on age, sex, language, location and even income don't actually deliver an accurate picture of a constantly shifting audience for technology products. So IBM defined groups of consumers by capturing attitudes,

Table 2.2 Segmentation of audiences by adoption of emerging technologies[14]

Babyboomers	Generation X	Generation Y	Net Generation	Mobile Generation
Average age is 55.	Average age is 29	Average age is 18.	Average age is 15.	Average age is 8.
By the age of 30 years technologies were beginning to take off.	First generation to experience new consumer technologies like PCs, video computer games, 24-hour news, CDs, satellite TV, mobile phones (related to business use) and personal digital assistants (PDAs).	This generation experienced a childhood that was filled with early editions of modern technologies.	This generation has had exposure to the greatest number of consumer technologies in history.	This generation will experience true transparency of technological interfaces and ubiquitous communication.
They were the entrepreneurs who first dictated and pushed evolution of modern technologies; 40% now have pay TV at home.	Key values are individualism and self-fulfilment. They are adaptable, culturally astute, commercially savvy, and highly brand aware.	Palmtop computers, cable TV, console gaming games, the World Wide Web, mobile phones, digital cameras, e-commerce, digital TV and the ubiquitous PC were becoming common commodites.	The speed and complexity of the technology market is being harnessed and exploited by them. They are confident, voracious and experimental towards technology.	Already accustomed to technologies at the 'bleeding' edge, they will experience and shape G3 (next generation technologies), MMS (Multimedia Messaging Service, (XDAs (hand held computer and Web tool).
A quarter are active computer users and they use technology in work and play.	This is a generation used to coping with new technologies, more keyed into fashion and design and will probably keep this habit into their old age.	They witnessed the launch of 'Space Invaders' and 'Pac Man'.	Many have become accustomed to Windows, PowerMacs, e-mail, Playstation, palmtop computers, mobile phones, WAP, text messaging and broadband.	Games include MMORPGS (Massively Multiplayer Online Role Playing Games), moving to pervasive gaming or games that 'play you'.

Table 2.2 *continued*

They exploit their prosperity.	Technology was moving forward with speed and many big companies marketed to a growing consumer base.	Sony Playstation was released in the US. The gaming experience was further enhanced by the introduction of joysticks and steering wheels. 'Wing Commander III' and 'Heart of the Tiger' were released which featured for the first time full motion video. 'Barbie: Fashion Designer' was launched and created a new generation of girl gamers.	They differ from the Net Generation, who see the Web as 'virtual' whereas the Mobile Generation see the Web as 'portable'.
80% use word processing applications for letter writing and nearly 60% send and receive e-mails on a regular basis.			This generation will witness the convergence of Web and mobile. Distinctions between virtual, real and the third space (the perceived gap between on- and off-line environments) will disappear.

beliefs and behaviours as a way of segmenting its audience according to the propensity to use technology.

The public relations programme therefore reflects exactly the issues that have an influence on changing attitudes, beliefs and behaviours of each of those segments and in this way public relations opportunities are leveraged for maximum efficiency. As a result of this focus, public relations can deliver a distinctive proposition as part of the marketing communications plan that is tailored to the needs of each of these individual groups.

THE MARKETING COMMUNICATIONS PLAN

A simple marketing communications plan will contain the following elements:

- *Background*. Why are we preparing this document? What do we want this document to achieve?
- *Segmentation of target audiences*. Who are we trying to reach? What do we know about them?
- *Critical success factors*. What are the key things we need to achieve in order for this plan to be a success?
- *Market research*. What are our strategies based on? (Summarize research in bullet points.)
- *Internal analysis*. What within my organization can affect this plan, both positively and negatively?
- *Environmental analysis*. What factors in my environment can affect my purpose? What changes must we plan for? (State the assumptions you are making about the future.)
- *Competitor analysis*. Who are our competitors?
- *Marketing SWOT analysis*. What factors are hindering or restraining our purpose? What environmental factors are driving or assisting our purpose? (List here your strengths, weaknesses, opportunities and threats.)
- *Marketing objectives*. Where do we want to go? What does the business or organization want to achieve and by when?
- *Marketing strategies*. How are we going to get there? (Put these in bullet points.)
- *Evaluation and measurement*. How will we know that we have achieved our objective? (Indicate how you will evaluate, measure and report against your key quantification mechanisms.)

- *Master timetable and action list.* When will we get there? (Map strategies against time frames and responsibilities of individuals for delivering the plan.)
- *Resources.* Usually entered on a spreadsheet clearly indicating likely costs for all the elements of the marketing plan and other pertinent financial information such as labour costs and technology costs.

CASE STUDY: LAUNCH OF THE UK'S FIRST PRIVATE ONCOLOGY CLINICAL TRIALS CENTRE

This example brings together the various elements of a successful marketing communications plan and shows the pivotal role that PR plays within the marketing context.

BACKGROUND

- Early days for the joint venture for the clinical trials centre (between two major USA-based healthcare groups).
- 'Clean sheet' – details including brand name still to be agreed.
- Business feasibility study sets down some critical success factors for the new clinical trials centre.
- Resistance and competitive threats to the project.
- Competitor research required.
- Lead in time for unit operation is at least 18 months.
- Proactive approach to marketing and communications essential in order to keep interest alive prior to opening of the centre.

SEGMENTATION OF TARGET AUDIENCES

- Patients.
- Clinicians.
- Medical and oncological establishments.
- Government (Department of Health).
- Pharmaceutical industry.
- Biotech companies.
- International and national news media.
- Scientific and medical media.
- Business press.
- Academic community.

CRITICAL SUCCESS FACTORS

- Highly competitive pricing.
- High volume, secure patient access.
- Top-drawer principal investigators.
- Audited facilities for the conduct of Phase I and II clinical trials.
- Relationships with 11 major pharmaceutical and biotech companies in the UK.

MARKET RESEARCH

- Phase I and II Units in the US, UK, Ireland, France, Germany, the Netherlands and Spain.
- Pricing models.
- Ten NHS Clinical Trials Units supported by NTRAC.

INTERNAL ANALYSIS

- No current name for the joint venture.
- Brand identity issues.
- Appointment of board of directors.
- Articles and memorandum of association.
- Type of cancer drugs that the clinical trials centre will investigate.
- Business plan for the new centre.
- Scope for licensing the brand in other territories.

ENVIRONMENTAL ANALYSIS

- Legal and regulatory environment in England and Wales.
- Threats from NTRAC and National Transitional Cancer Research Network.
- Patient groups.
- Cancer charities.
- Political parties.
- Medicines Control Agency.

COMPETITOR ANALYSIS

- Phase I and II Units in the US, UK, Ireland, France, Germany, the Netherlands and Spain.

- Pricing models.
- Ten NHS Clinical Trials Units supported by NTRAC.

SWOT ANALYSIS

- Strengths include leadership, resources and central London location.
- Weaknesses include Government and Department of Health attitude to clinical trials in the private sector.
- Opportunities include creating the largest privately-run cancer clinical trials centre in the UK.
- Threats include not competing on value and price with other clinical trials centres in the US and mainland Europe.

MARKETING OBJECTIVES

- Create, support, promote and enhance the new brand in the UK.
- Start to create a 'climate change' where the role of the private sector in clinical trials is acceptable rather than unusual.
- Promote the voices of third parties to deliver key messages.
- Create a position of thought leadership for the unit and its leaders.
- Win the hearts and minds of patients, clinicians, the medical/oncological establishment and Government.
- Assist in winning the largest number of Phase I/II studies from big pharmaceutical and biotech companies.
- Assist in achieving the highest number of drug candidates in the world for a unit of this type.
- Assist in achieving the highest patient recruitment rate for any comparable unit in Europe.
- To be renowned as a centre of excellence by the medical profession worldwide.

MARKETING STRATEGIES

- Public relations (relationship building) programme.
- Opinion leaders programme.
- Roundtable programme.
- Strengthening relationships with:
  - National Cancer Research Network
  - National Translational Cancer Research Network

- NTRAC
- Royal Marsden
- Department of Health
- Prime Minister's Office
- Conservative and Liberal Democrat health spokespersons
- Office of the Mayor of London
- others…
- Media relations:
  - national news media
  - international news media.
- Specialist publications:
  - health sector
  - public sector
  - patient publications
  - cancer journals
  - business journals
  - charity titles
  - others…
- Paperback book: *Positive Action: A comprehensive guide to partici-pating in clinical trials:*
  - aimed at patients, clinicians, regulatory and research profes-sionals in oncology
  - detailed review of the European oncological clinical trials process
  - differences in clinical trials between European countries and the UK
  - how to determine if a clinical trial is suitable
  - evaluation of current clinical trials
  - special considerations
  - useful checklist and reference to further information.
- Academic links:
  - tie up with leading business schools in Europe and US: Insead, Judge Institute/MIT, London Business School, Harvard, Kellogg, Yale
  - proprietary research can help drive the PR effort
  - thought leadership – also feeds into opinion leaders programme and roundtable programme
  - relationship with World Health Organization and IARC.
- White papers:
  - economics of clinical trials
  - delivery of quality clinical trials at an affordable cost
  - best practice global research on clinical trials
  - views and fears of patients and clinicians in taking part in clinical trials

- – the recruitment of suitable patients for Phase I/II clinical trials
- – what big pharmaceutical and biotech companies should look for in early phase studies
- – the role of technology in clinical trials
- – etc...
- Web site:
  - – a portal for latest news and information on cancer
  - – up-to-date information on patient groups and links to other Web sites
  - – online guide for patients, families and friends on clinical trials
  - – update on the development of the unit in Harley Street with a Web cam update
  - – chat room and notice board
  - – public opinion surveys
  - – useful search facility for articles on cancer
  - – recruitment survey.
- Sponsorship:
  - – patient information/patient groups
  - – educational (clinicians)
  - – broadcast (cable/satellite health programme)
  - – cultural/photographic/arts exhibitions
  - – national and European conferences/symposiums
  - – university chair in Clinical Oncology.

EVALUATION AND MEASUREMENT

- Delivery of the marketing communications programme on time and within budget.
- Positive feedback from the opinion leaders and roundtable programme.
- Positive news coverage of the plans for the new clinical trials centre in the national and international media, with no negative messages.
- Public support from patient groups and clinicians.
- Acceptance and participation in public relations from NTRAC and Department of Health.
- Joint public relations with cancer charities, eg Royal Marsden Hospital.

The timetable and resources for this activity are shown in Table 2.3.

Table 2.3 *Timetable and resources*

Activity	Timing	Approx Consultancy Days	Costs
Brand identity Working with a design agency	June/July	7	£000s
Competitor research	June/July	4	£000s
Marketing and communications strategy and plan	June/July	5	£000s
Opinion leaders programme identification, set up database Time input can be reduced with support	September	4 days per month	£000s
Roundtable programme identification, set up database Time input can be reduced with support	September	4 days per month	£000s
Web site Managing and working with IT and Web design team	June/July	5	£000s
White papers Research, writing, editing, revising	Once a quarter	5–7 per paper	£000s
Paperback book	June/July (coincide with opening of the unit in 2004)	Further discussion required	£000s
Media relations	September/ October	2–4 days per month	£000s
Sponsorship Search for four suitable sponsorship properties and manage these	May December June 2004 December 2004	Further discussion required	£000s
Academic links	June/July	1 day per month	£000s
Conferences, seminars, events	November 2003 onwards	Further discussion required	£000s

As this case study vividly demonstrates, PR is an essential component of the marketing communications mix and the whole project could not gain credibility without it.

THE NEW MARKETING PARADIGM

Fragmentation of media and of audiences has delivered a wake-up call to most brand owners and organizations in terms of the effectiveness of their marketing communications activities. Advertising in particular is failing to deliver cut-through with media savvy audiences who can screen out messages with ease. In the future there are likely to be more technologies that enable consumers to make choices for themselves. This not only allows them to record their favourite TV programmes by skipping the ad breaks but also enables them to create their own TV programmes. The next 20 years will be the most challenging for brand owners and organizations as they start to grapple with this dynamic environment where the balance of power has firmly switched to the audience.

The net result of all these changes is the increasing importance of public relations in marketing communications where genuine understanding and dialogue will pay dividends for those who need to win hearts and minds. The future of public relations practice is rapidly evolving to embrace these challenges and we're likely to see more resources switched into public relations programmes and away from 'hard sell' marketing techniques such as promotions and competitions, advertising and Web-based communication, which is becoming ever more intrusive.

Unlike the efforts of Mr Sahhaf, tomorrow's public relations practitioners will use public relations in order to engage in meaningful dialogue as well as influence changes in behaviour, both externally as well as internally.

Public relations has moved centre stage within marketing communications as the new marketing paradigm.

Checklist

The following checklist will act as an aide memoire of the key points of this chapter:

- Never make assumptions without knowing the full facts. This is guaranteed to damage any marketing communications programme and the reputation of the brand owner or organization.
- Appreciate the legal context for marketing communications.
- Statistics and research are useful, but over-reliance on research is dangerous. Always take into account other evidence in order to reach a conclusion or decision.
- Always segment the key audiences (include behaviours as part of this process), even if the audiences appear to be homogenous.
- Make sure that the marketing communication strategy and plan meet measurable business and organizational objectives. If they don't, they will fail to deliver value.
- Public relations, as part of marketing communications, is a channel of communication in its own right. Public relations also supports other channels of communication, so make sure that public relations fits within the context of the total marketing communications mix.
- Successful public relations within the context of marketing communications is a combination of:
  - listening to the audience;
  - considering their needs, hopes, desires, dreams;
  - acting in an appropriate way that meets these requirements (and paying attention to the tone of communication);
  - measuring the impact of communications (in terms of behaviours);
  - evaluating this in terms of hard measures (eg sales);
  - reviewing the net result in order to shape future public relations activities.
- Ultimately the communication process will impact on the perceptions and behaviours of all parties and therefore effective public relations is a two-way process.
- Purchasing decisions are made on two levels: the rational and the emotional. Because of the way in which the human brain works, it's emotion that sells (a key point of differentiation where a consumer is faced with choosing two almost identical products or services).
- Always review the tools of communication, including the use of the Web, mobile and interactive platforms. But remember

> that face-to-face communication may not be effectively substituted in all cases.
> - Always consider the financial implications of marketing communications and ensure that there is a reasonable return on investment (ROI), which should also take account of staff time and overheads of the brand owner or organization.

Notes

1. DTI/IPR Steering Group, March 2003.
2. www.ipr.org.uk.
3. Ries, A and Ries, L (2002) *The Fall of Advertising and the Rise of PR*, Harper Collins, New York.
4. Kotler, P, 'Public Relations versus Marketing: Dividing the Conceptual Domain and Operational Turf.' Position paper for the Public Relations Colloquium 1989, San Diego, USA.
5. Ibid.
6. Ambler, T, London Business School, October 2002.
7. American Marketing Association, 1985.
8. Under the revised *British Code of Advertising, Sales Promotion and Direct Marketing* 2003 (CAP Code), if there is an objective piece of research or a genuine independent opinion from a bona fide published source, say a magazine like *Which?*, then the CAP Code permits use of this statement without the need to obtain permission from the author. The caveat is: 'Unless they are genuine statements taken from a published source, references to tests, trials, professional endorsements, research facilities and professional journals should be used only with the permission of those concerned.'
9. Sachs, M (1996) 'Marketing Communications', in *Public Relations in Practice*, 1st edition, Kogan Page, London.
10. This activity is caught by the *British Code of Advertising, Sales Promotion and Direct Marketing* (www.cap.org.uk) as well as the Data Protection Act 1998 (see Kolah, A (2002) *Essential Law for Marketers*, Butterworth-Heinemann).
11. Ridderstråle, J and Nordström, K (2000) *Funky Business*, Book House Publishing AB, Stockholm.
12. In terms of consumers, this means effecting an increase in the propensity to consume a product or service (which is a useful financial measure). In terms of non-consumers, this means achieving a particular desired outcome (for example, a change of perception and behaviour – which is a useful non-financial measure).
13. Klein, N (2001) *No Logo*, Flamingo.
14. Agents of Change (2003) is a major research study by IBM's Interactive Media in Retail Group.

3

Internal communication

Pamela Mounter

Internal communication used to be the poor relation of a business. At best it meant a house journal, at worst an out-of-date memo on a notice board no one admitted owning. When one major oil company started looking at ways to improve internal communication in its refining and marketing business, a senior manager commented: 'Don't they read the papers?'

How many managers do we know who are happy to talk to analysts and the press but not to their staff? Yet successful businesses know they need effective internal communication to get employees aligned with company goals. It's a tool just as much as financial analysis. Internal communication is *not* a soft issue.

The two case studies concluding this chapter, one relating to a National Health Trust, one to a European conglomerate, show that internal communication does have an impact on performance. While the NHS example relates to a new organization starting with a clean sheet of paper, the European conglomerate study describes how an established business was broken up. The challenges were therefore rather different. What unites them is ownership of the issues by all concerned, facilitated by good listening processes.

WHY COMMUNICATE?

Today the average employee expects more from his or her leader than a pay cheque. Companies need to engage their employees in improving the business. But if employees don't know what they are doing and why, they are less likely to work effectively. A properly planned and executed communication strategy motivates employees. It's the corporate glue that helps build teams, reinforces pride in working for a company and encourages people to work that bit harder to beat the competition (see Figure 3.1). It cuts the crap out of the process. It will:

- provide a source of performance improvement;
- bridge the gap between functions and departments;
- disseminate best practice;
- provide rich context; and
- track progress.

Communication is the link between an organization's compelling need for change and an employee's compelling need for security. In 2002 Hill and Knowlton, the public affairs consultancy, asked

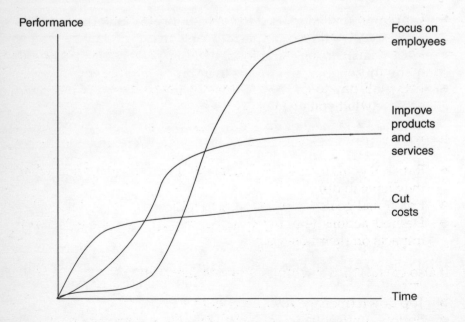

Figure 3.1 *Sources of performance improvement*

chief executives to rank their top priorities. Employee communication came second, after addressing company change. The two are of course inextricably linked.

Now we're in the recession-hit noughties even McDonald's is starting to focus more closely on internal communication and create processes for capturing what employees think. The catalyst was the company's first ever loss. With the share price dropping and a brand audit where McDonald's received feedback like 'arrogant', 'don't listen' and 'they tell us what we're going to have' the company's confidence was knocked. In the UK they took action by appointing their first internal communication manager – and listening to their staff.

TELLING – AND LISTENING

That word 'listening' is fundamental to communication. Communication is a two-way process involving listening at least as much as telling. The word comes from the Latin *communicare*, meaning to share. Information shared falls into three main categories:

- Corporate: builds pride and belonging ('I am proud to work for and feel good about my company').
- Cascade: communicates objectives ('What you want me to do and why').
- Personal: day-to-day motivation ('How you persuade me to achieve what you want me to do').

It covers:

- Rational goals (employees understand their business and what they have to do).
- Emotional goals (employees are involved).
- Desired actions (employees understand how their behaviour impacts on their business).

It also creates the right attitude by communicating:

- Top down (management message).
- Bottom up (feedback, not just on those messages but on what is concerning staff right now).

- Laterally (across functions, welding the organization into one team).

When it's working well people are encouraged to say what they think about the information they have been given and they can see that what they have said makes a difference. And when people see management taking action on their feedback, the whole process gains trust and credibility, as the National Health Trust example later on shows.

WIN MANAGEMENT COMMITMENT

So where do you begin? The two case studies show how essential is senior management commitment. Internal communication only works when managers and employees are involved. The challenge is that senior managers – the people with the real responsibility for internal communication – feel they don't have time for it.

When BP's refining and marketing business went through a massive downsizing in the early 1990s its senior managers, spread around the world, were far from convinced that internal communication, those so important messages from head office, had anything to do with them. 'When I get those little pieces of paper from head office I put them into a drawer until they are dead,' said one.

The trick was to involve them in something they would find useful. In Europe, for example, they identified what makes a good communicator by comparing results from an attitude survey with staff and management interviews. To many people's surprise they discovered that it's all about attitude rather than natural talent and that encouraged them (see Figure 3.2).

In the Far East they mapped the communication processes. Simply identifying who did what helped focus hearts and minds on the subject. As an additional benefit, the results of these projects were publicized around the BP world through the newly formed network of communicators who championed them as best practice. So Thailand adopted the 'brown bag' informal lunch concept of the US in a very Thai way. To beat the hierarchical Thai office system, the chief executive simply invited everyone with a birthday that month to join him for lunch, the only way he could get forklift truck drivers and accountants sitting down together.

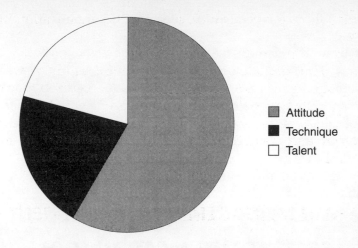

Figure 3.2 *Creating the right attitude*

You have to watch, however, that your managers don't start over-communicating. In the interests of openness, managers in one company with its back to the wall started speculating with their staff about what might happen. That was not communication but frankly lack of leadership. It led to massive uncertainty until the chief executive stepped smartly in and stopped it.

Once you have management commitment – but you have to earn it – you can then take that crucial first step of carrying out research to benchmark attitudes, issues and opportunities, to find out what needs fixing. What you don't know can hurt you. That might be an all-employee survey and/or a series of focus groups to uncover issues and identify different cultural nuances. It visibly demonstrates that the company cares about what its employees think.

Meanwhile work can begin on defining the few messages that really matter to the business. The emphasis is on few – too many and people switch off. That's where internal communication managers will need to use all their diplomatic skills to reassure senior managers they are included in the process of defining what really counts. Those skills are also needed to craft the words in readily understood language, free from business jargon. One good test is to ask yourself: Would an intelligent 12-year-old child understand this? Because that's who you should be aiming at.

Here's a four-step checklist for defining the message:

1. Analyse the business plan.
2. Translate the high level concepts into readily understood language.
3. Identify the various internal audiences.
4. 'Road-test' the messages derived from the business plan with the various audiences to make sure they are understood.

Then deliver the messages through a combination of the tools available.

SOME COMMUNICATION TOOLS

Read any attitude survey and it will say people prefer face-to-face communication. But how practical is it? Some managers are very uncomfortable with internal communication. They feel they don't have time for it – 'I've got a business to run' – and they don't know how to handle the feedback, listening part of it. These are not insuperable challenges but they do require resources, not least for managers who may need coaching in talking effectively to their teams.

Face-to-face or primary communication includes:

●   senior management briefings;
●   senior management 'road shows' and lunches;
●   employee forums;
●   team briefings;
●   focus groups;
●   award schemes.

Focus groups seem to have fallen out of fashion but they do give employees the chance to provide feedback in a 'safe' environment.

Secondary communication tools, ie not face-to-face, include:

●   e-mail;
●   intranet;
●   employee publications;
●   video and audio conferencing;
●   surveys and questionnaires.

Use the right tool for the job. E-mail and the intranet are excellent for rapid communication. US appliance controls company Invensys, for example, briefs employees via an e-mail alert with a hotlink to the company intranet, to the latest update from the chief executive. This appears in two forms, one to be read on screen and one to be printed off. House journals and videos can provide in-depth background and context.

THE FEEDBACK LOOP

Now comes the real challenge: how do you know if the message has landed – and what do employees think of it? Be aware that some managers fear feedback because they feel it reflects on their performance. A non-threatening way to deliver feedback is:

- say what you like;
- say what you don't like and why;
- suggest ways of dealing with the 'don't like'.

How you collect feedback will depend on the individual company or location. Paper questionnaires and surveys are one answer – but employees rightly resent constant surveys. A short and sweet 'tick box' or 'yes/no' questionnaire has a better chance of being answered than a long one that asks for the reader's written opinions. Other options include the facility to comment by e-mail on intranet briefs, intranet discussion groups and forums, telephone surveys and focus groups.

Whichever route you choose, it is essential to report back to employees on the findings, and action taken on the findings. If there are good commercial reasons for not being able to take action, say so and why.

All communication needs to be repeated and reinforced: messages need to be repeated, and repeated over time through the intelligent use of the various tools; see Figure 3.3.

MEASURES OF SUCCESS

So how do you know if you're getting it right? How to measure success will be for the internal communication manager to negotiate with senior management.

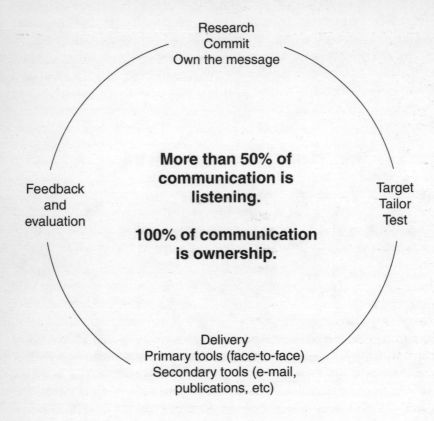

Figure 3.3 *The virtuous circle of communication*

Here are the four key questions, the criteria for measuring success:

1. Have we identified the issues?
2. Have we created a feedback programme?
3. Have we created an ongoing dialogue between employees and management?
4. Have we engaged the board?

Here are some suggestions on how to measure that success:

- employee attitude surveys;
- planned production of an agreed number of briefs/ journals/roadshows;

- responses to articles in house journals;
- feedback on team briefings;
- questionnaires;
- focus groups;
- number of hits on intranet briefs;
- reward schemes.

The Institute of Public Relations publishes a useful research and evaluation toolkit ('Planning, Research and Evaluation Toolkit', IPR, 2003) which, while aimed at public relations practitioners, has lessons for internal communication: both require a structured, disciplined approach.

SUPPORT NETWORKS

The IPR also has a special interest group dedicated to internal communication. The value of groups like this is that members are drawn from different industries. They can provide fresh thinking on common issues such as: 'How do I get my managers to support internal communication?'

The debate about where internal communication should sit – usually a tussle between Human Resources and Public Relations – is to my mind irrelevant. Both should be wooed for support, HR with training, feedback and analysis and PR with audience targeting and wordsmithing. Internal communication and PR need to liaise closely so that messages given internally do not conflict with those published externally.

In large organizations with several locations, consider setting up a network of communication champions to support their managers. BP did this successfully by asking the managers themselves to nominate their champions, so both the champions and the managers owned the outcomes. Other sources of support include industry benchmarking and external advisers.

COMMUNICATION BEST PRACTICE

Here are some useful ideas from a communication review of one company that drastically shrank its head office:

- Use face-to-face communication by line management as the primary method of communication (seek training if necessary).
- Involve 'professional communicators' at the outset and throughout to help identify the messages, deliver them in the appropriate way to the various targeted audiences and to provide feedback on how well the messages have been understood (and to provide feedback on grassroots concerns about them).
- Explain and establish the business case for the event to staff.
- Identify and communicate the positive changes that will result from the event.
- Coordinate the timing of communications to staff in different teams to avoid potentially demoralizing rumours spreading in advance of the formal announcement.
- Do not speculate: this leads to increased uncertainty among staff.
- Allow as much time as it takes for people to talk through whatever they want to talk about.
- Communicate with staff in a clear, honest, consistent and timely manner.
- Own the message.

IN SUMMARY...

Effective communication is about telling people where they are going (message, top down), welding the different parts of the organization into one team (delivery, horizontal) and getting information on how well communication is working (feedback, bottom up). Seven steps to communication heaven are:

1. commitment of senior management;
2. evaluation/research of issues, local and global;
3. identification of the few, really important, messages;
4. creation of some form of network of communication champions to support local management;
5. agreement on the non-negotiables concerning delivery and feedback;
6. empowerment and ownership of local management and its support network/s;
7. engagement at all levels in a continuing process.

Internal communication is a shared resource. It is not, as some think, something done to them. Nor is it, as some managers think, something that people do for them. Good internal communication treats people as an end in themselves, not as a means to an end.

CASE STUDY: NHS TRUST

When this Trust was set up it had to win agreement from its multiple stakeholders on the way forward. What made this particularly challenging was that it was a Trust providing services for people with a mental health or learning disabilities problem. Stakeholders included:

- service users and carers;
- voluntary organizations;
- advocacy organizations;
- self-help groups;
- staff;
- staff representatives;
- Community Health Councils;
- Primary Care Trusts;
- local authorities; and
- executive and non-executive directors.

The chief executive began a series of 'listening' workshops to encourage staff and stakeholders to talk about what the organization should stand for, what service they expected from it and how best to communicate with all the people involved. This was articulated as the Trust's vision, values and goals and expressed as:

- what we were trying to achieve (vision);
- how we would behave on the way (values);
- what we should do to move us to where we want to be (goals).

In preparation, the chief executive produced a draft setting out the Trust's direction and goals using comments from the original consultation process for setting up the Trust and information gathered from visits throughout the service and discussions with staff and stakeholder groups.

To start the process the Trust ran one large workshop for multiple stakeholders. In all, 125 people attended, including 40 members of staff. Issues teased out of that workshop were then taken to five workshops – across all four localities – for staff. Finally, another multiple stakeholder workshop was held to feedback the finalized vision, values and goals.

While there was a good match between the draft vision and values and the themes and comments at the listening events, there were some significant additions. On vision for example, people wanted to include the goal of supporting staff. On values, they asked for an explicit recognition of the organization having a focus on learning and improvement. On a practical issue, the workshops highlighted the need to standardize policies across the four localities. Statutory training, for example, merited a pass/fail certificate in one area and a simple certificate of attendance in another.

These workshops were a stunning success. People particularly appreciated the multi-stakeholder nature of some of them and welcomed the chance to share ideas across the whole patch.

Among the communication tools now being considered are a staff magazine, local newsletters, a newsletter for carers, board member road shows and an anonymous question and answer facility accessible to all staff, service users and carers. Meanwhile the Trust is proactively using the media to champion mental health and learning disability issues.

To one of the non-executive directors one of the most surprising results of the listening process was the universal agreement that one of the Trust's primary aims was to champion equality. She had expected a statement about service to top the list. By championing equality the stakeholders committed themselves to promoting opportunities for people with mental health problems or learning disabilities. That included:

- publicizing their positive achievements and images;
- championing the need to combat discrimination against them;
- social inclusion; and
- using the specialist knowledge of people in the Trust to influence local and national views.

The full Trust vision now reads:

South West Yorkshire Mental Health NHS Trust… sound organization, supported workers, working through partnership to:

- *champion equality;*
- *encourage involvement;*
- *support and value diverse lives;*
- *modernize services and increase choice;*

for people with a learning disability and people with mental health problems and their carers.

This, interestingly, reverses the order of the two final bullet points in the draft version produced for the workshops.

The first tangible output is an attractive and user-friendly booklet setting out the Trust's agreed vision, values and goals. It is available in languages other than English and also in Braille, large print and on audiotape. It includes the following feedback invitation:

> These statements will be reviewed thoroughly on an annual basis and the Trust welcomes your comments and suggestions. If you would like to comment, or be involved in the future development of these statements, please use the contact details given below.

CASE STUDY: EUROPEAN CONGLOMERATE MARKETING EXIT

BACKGROUND

The European marketing and distribution operation for an international company delivered bulk products to millions of customers, ranging from small commercial and light industrial customers with deliveries once or twice a year to large industrial customers with deliveries several times a day. Some were handled by small distributors, others by company-operated facilities.

A few years ago the business was reorganized into call centres and procedures standardized in the interests of efficiency. However, each country implemented the plan differently. The new procedures added complexity rather than making the business more efficient. After two years head office issued a very clear instruction: sell the parts of the business that you can and shut down the rest.

Normally this would be handled by packaging the business as an entity, doing secret negotiations with potential buyers, then announcing the sale when everything was cut and dried. But this business was not marketable as a whole, the potential buyers being very small companies. It had to be split into some 40 packages to attract potential buyers, not a process that could be kept secret or executed quickly. Also, the business had to be kept going while it was being sold – the only asset of any value was the customer list and the delivery operation. Lose the customers or the staff and the business became worthless.

The challenge for the communication strategy was to keep a diverse group of staff motivated for a couple of years while parts were being sold. That would be difficult even in a single country. The task was to do this with 4,000 staff spread across 10 countries, and to communicate with each of them in a way that made sense in their own culture and for their particular business.

WHAT DID THEY DO?

First, communication was recognized as a key success factor for the project. A senior business manager with a good track record in dealing with such issues was appointed to the project team to manage it. A network of communication managers in each country supported him. In parallel a network of Human Resources managers was set up to deal with people issues and employment law. Those two networks worked in close harmony throughout the project, using frequent audio conferences and position papers to keep aligned.

Secondly, a bonus plan was set up for all the business line managers, with reputation and people management as the main performance criteria. Thirdly, a communication strategy was devised with the following characteristics:

- Line managers to engage in frequent dialogue with staff and listen to staff concerns even if there is no news to tell them.
- Over-communicate news to those directly affected but under-communicate news to others; always communicate news via line managers.
- Give staff time to come to terms with one piece of news before delivering the next.
- Take full account of national/cultural issues and differentiate style and timing of messages in different countries.
- Manage the whole process with military precision.

THE ISSUES

The first big issue was the 'We've screwed up' message inherent in the situation. The business had gone through a painful reorganization which hadn't worked and people felt a failure. Someone was to blame. Fortunately some instigators of the reorganization had moved on. The new managers could represent themselves as 'part of the solution' rather than 'part of the problem'. Different ways of implementing the strategy could be presented as evidence that staff in each country knew what was best for it. The new way forward could be presented as local empowerment, so people felt part of the solution.

This led to the next question: 'Why should the new solution be any better than the last time?' The communication plan focused on the context and process of evaluating options. It emphasized that different options played differently in different countries, helping convince staff this was not a 'one size fits all' approach. Local staff felt ownership of local solutions. Focusing news on those affected reinforced the process.

International rivalry played a big part and with people working under intense pressure it's perhaps not surprising some conformed to their national stereotypes:

- the English were happy with fairly vague plans so long as their plans were announced before the French ones and they could demonstrate leadership;
- the Scots didn't mind what happened to them so long as it was different to the English outcome;
- the Belgians were happy to have any solution that they could blame on the French or Germans;
- the Swiss fixed their solution quietly while no one else was watching.

EU employment law requires pan-European consultation of cross-national business changes with significant social impact. Negotiating so many disparate local deals with a European Works Council would have been impossible. So the general context was dealt with at the European level, the detail at local level.

There was considerable concern that announcements in one country would be seen as the 'writing on the wall' for other countries. However, early communication of the context – explaining the problems facing the business – helped give people time to get used to the need for radical change. Announcements in other countries did raise concerns but were seen in proper context. There was also a conscious effort to schedule the lesser social consequence deals early, to acclimatize people for the more devastating deals to come.

WHAT'S IN A WORD?

Words have different meanings in different places. People have an infinite capacity to misunderstand messages, particularly in a multicultural situation. So the communication network scrutinized absolutely everything to iron out all the negative nuances in the different cultures.

Finally, the team had to manage the desire of main board directors to tell shareholders what a good job they had done. Yet success depended on messaging the process as a series of minor local events. 'Claiming the credit' would have undermined it completely. Directors were carefully coached on the fact that they risked destroying success with a wrong message.

DID IT WORK?

The business was sold, all staff were treated with dignity and the managers got their bonuses.

4

Financial public relations

Terrence Collis

The ups and downs of stock markets, economic miracles and economic crises, pension 'black holes', boom dot coms – all mixed in with a regular cycle of business scandals – have helped ensure that financial public relations plays a major role, not only in business activity, but also in many people's daily lives.

So, for reasons good and bad, the importance of financial public relations continues to grow. Volatile stock markets and the next round of corporate fraud have meant a steadily increasing demand for greater corporate transparency and more understandable information about business activity. This demand for information is driven not only by the owners of businesses – the shareholders – but also by a whole range of other audiences now collectively known as 'stakeholders'. It is difficult for a business to carry out any activity without tripping over a stakeholder of one sort or another including staff, 'the community', special interest groups and regulators.

As a result, the media's appetite for business news seems to have no limit. In the UK some 10 or so national daily newspapers, a similar number of national Sunday papers, not to mention regional newspapers, regularly cover business and financial matters. In addition, there is a multitude of specialist publications incorporating the words 'money' or 'finance' in their title. The airwaves also contain an array of national and international satellite, cable and terrestrial television channels, hundreds of radio stations and the result is ever-growing coverage of corporate, industrial, business and consumer affairs.

Pensions, investments and savings have also become a more important, and more controversial, factor in many peoples' lives. With most of the developed world bemoaning savings gaps and pensions 'black holes', the subject of personal finance has ceased to be a minority interest. All this takes up more and more pages of print and more and more hours of airtime – and makes work for financial public relations specialists.

HOW DO YOU DEFINE FINANCIAL PUBLIC RELATIONS?

In common with the rest of the public relations industry, financial public relations people suffer from an inability to define their jobs. Some simply like to state that financial public relations all comes down to money – but that could be said for the vast majority of public relations activities. With significant sums of money and corporate resources dedicated to financial communication, we should at least be able to define the sort of return we expect for our investment in the activity.

This chapter looks at financial public relations from the UK, and primarily medium to large company, point of view. However, as the emphasis is on how basic communication skills and clear understanding of messages applies to financial communication most comments should apply equally to businesses of any size.

The commercial and social environment has changed. As a result the narrow focus on shareholders – that was for a long time the simple objective of most financial communications – is no longer an option for most companies. The growing importance of other stakeholders to the long-term success of a business has led to a more sophisticated and balanced approach to public relations and public affairs activities.

However, shareholders and the financial success of the company remain at the heart of any corporate public relations planning. Maintaining the support of other stakeholders is a key aim, but it is a key aim not in itself but in order to achieve the financial returns that the shareholders of a company – the owners – expect.

Shareholders, staff and customers are much more likely to be supportive of a company with a good reputation for integrity and honesty not only for financial success. Clarity and openness in communication, a clear strategy and a respected leadership also add to a company's reputation.

The primary focus remains the shareholders and those who advise them. The skills of financial public relations people are therefore largely focused on the need for publicly owned and listed companies to communicate consistently and positively with those that own them. The majority of the effort put into this specialist area of public relations surrounds the biannual issuing of results by companies, directly or indirectly, through the media or through City analysts.

For many millions of companies, large and small, around the world, the prosaic necessity of getting a proper understanding of their full-year and half-year figures is the most important part of any financial public relations strategy. Increasingly there are also important announcements made at other times of the year, such as quarterly reporting of results or regular updates on key factors such as production levels for oil companies, passenger loading for airlines, key Christmas or summer sales figures for retailers, or regulatory approvals for pharmaceutical companies. The management of these announcements and the management of the market's anticipation of them make up much of the direct financial communications activity of large organizations.

MERGERS AND ACQUISITIONS

The hectic activity that surrounds major bids, deals and financial disasters is more dramatic, more newsworthy and more likely to be the subject of airport paperbacks, but the majority of this work has as much to do with crisis management activity as it does with financial public relations. Happily for those who enjoy working in the financial public relations arena, the opening up and deregulation of world stock markets and the freeing up of international capital has made merger and acquisition work a significant part of financial public relations for the last two decades.

The economic cycle and the ups and downs of the stock market do produce quiet periods in merger and acquisition activities. These tend to coincide with difficult market conditions and communications activity can conveniently switch to the financial crisis management and damage limitation communication that always accompany a harsher economic environment.

Stock markets and stock prices are inevitably a major focus of activity. The rules and regulations of the world stock and bond markets, and the complexity of accountancy standards, inevitably make financial public relations a complicated speciality. A few thousand words is not a lot in which to try and explain those complexities. In addition, financial public relations sits alongside investment relations and the two are sometimes combined. But it is simplest, perhaps, to talk of financial public relations as all the ways of communicating with a company's stakeholders – except the direct contact with shareholding institutions and analysts, which is the task of investor relations people and finance directors.

I concentrate chiefly on the UK and London market, which is as sophisticated as any in terms of both the equity market and the financial media. Experience shows the same skills and approach can be applied elsewhere in the world, even though the rules and regulations may differ considerably.

THE BASIC TASK

Day-to-day financial public relations, as opposed to the fizzy and more dramatic takeover bid, is a steady, long-term business dealing with a set calendar of events, the patient explanation of results, and what a company does and does not do.

However, as with any other piece of detailed information, a company's results are only meaningful against a background of understanding and an idea of what they mean for the future. If financial public relations were to be defined as purely the communication of sets of numbers to a highly specialized audience, life would be comparatively simple. However, we must always look at the wider picture.

As the majority of shareholders are the major stock-holding institutions rather than individual shareholders, it has become accepted that shareholders are talked about in inanimate terms of 'institutions' or 'funds'. But even institutions are run and managed by mere mortals, and their computer models are tools used by people with still at least a shred of humanity left. Financial public relations has to recognize that the managers who populate the investment institutions are affected by everything they see, read or hear about a company, its management, its reputation and its products. Financial public relations could, therefore, be taken to cover any aspect of public relations for a commercial organization.

Take for example a very large, very successful and truly international oil company such as BP, with a complex business and a range of activities in its portfolio: the presentation of each set of results or important announcement requires a high degree of careful planning. Even a company as closely followed and well known as BP has to be very focused about the messages it puts out with results, to ensure that those who follow the company understand the full significance of the numbers.

In particular this involves very careful preparation of the presentation to be given to both analysts and press. It is the views and the number crunching of the analysts that will influence the views of the other key audiences, including the financial press. Press and media briefings must be well coordinated. The key messages need to take into account other stakeholders in the organization, whether customers, staff, or community and environmental groups. BP, with a significant shareholding in the USA, also goes to great lengths to internationalize its announcements and to coordinate messages across the Atlantic and across the globe.

Such presentations cannot be given in a vacuum and are prepared in response to feedback on the various audiences' major concerns and areas of interest. By researching stakeholders' concerns in the period leading up to announcements the company can ensure it gets maximum value from the opportunity of its results presentations and anticipate and avoid future disclosure problems.

The tightening of rules on selective disclosure of information – designed to ensure that all shareholders have equal access to information – has made set piece announcements and presentations even more important to a company's communication programme. Anyone wishing to study the highest quality in terms of financial PR could do worse than learn from BP's work in this area.

Not all organizations appreciate the need for detailed communications planning. But it has become even more important than ever to take an opportunity – such as results – to put all significant information into the public arena through the approved channels. Failure to do this leads to being forced into a succession of additional announcements. The market rightly takes a dim view of those who cannot organize their communication effectively – particularly if the announcements are warnings of lower than expected profits!

CORPORATE PUBLIC RELATIONS

The twin areas of corporate and financial communication are inseparable. Corporate public relations and financial public relations are not merely close bedfellows, they are Siamese twins sharing the same vital activities.

Corporate public relations is usually defined as managing the reputation of the whole company – sometimes called the corporate brand. Often the single most influential component of this brand is the reputation of the senior management, usually the CEO or chairman. Certainly the media are keen to follow the cult of personality and often write as if running and owning a company are the same thing – as in 'Geoff Mulcahy's Kingfisher' or 'Martin Sorrell's WPP'. The corporate brand is not only important in terms of share performance but also involves other factors such as track record on corporate social responsibility or ethical policies.

With the growth of ethical investment funds and the growing influence of NGOs (Non-Governmental Organizations) and other pressure groups, these areas of public affairs are now important components of corporate and financial public relations. Corporate communications is all about enabling a company to succeed but success cannot be defined in simplistic financial terms.

Each to his own

Those who doubt the importance now given to corporate public relations by the key players in the City need only to consider the historic example of British Gas. A much-respected City commentator, writing in *The Times* about British Gas following an acrimonious annual general meeting in June 1995, concluded: 'The failure, as institutions perceive it, is not strategy but public relations. Fund managers have given the Board a few clear pointers about how this might be addressed.'

It is one of life's universal truths – along with the fact that nobody thinks they are a bad driver – that most people, whatever their profession, regard themselves as a public relations expert. Fund managers who feel they must give companies tips on their public relations will probably be relieved to hear that public relations people seldom seek to give advice on fund management.

It is also interesting to reflect that the outbreak of corporate scandals such as Enron and WorldCom have made people even more suspicious of slick presentation, spin and too much massaging of messages. The focus of any financial or corporate announcement should be on clarity and explanation rather than on spin and obfuscation.

The credibility of a management team takes a long time to build but is easily destroyed by careless or inaccurate communications. Once your audience starts to doubt your word all communication becomes difficult. Results and accounts, however, can be by their very nature complicated and obscure, even for the most straight-forward of companies.

WHAT CONTRIBUTION DOES FINANCIAL PUBLIC RELATIONS MAKE TO THE SUCCESS OF A COMPANY?

Some would argue that there is only one long-term measure of the success of financial public relations: share or bond price, or credit rating. There is no doubt that the majority of financial communication activity is aimed at creating more demand for shares in a particular company. Stimulate more buyers than sellers and share prices tend to rise.

There seems to be no reason why financial public relations should not be regarded as public relations support for a simple financial product – company shares. Although short-term success in increasing a share price may be welcome, ensuring that the City and City journalists have a clearer understanding of a company's strategy is far more important. The real contribution that good corporate and financial public relations makes to a company is in creating a clear understanding among financial audiences – of what that company really does and what it is trying to achieve, then making sure everyone knows when it meets or beats those objectives.

Monitoring and research are also essential if financial communication activity is to be properly measured. Not all monitoring and research is as accurate, cost-effective and useful as it might be. However, it is unwise to take a 'head in the sand' approach and judge the results of communication on instinct and gut feeling when there are clearly sensible, scientific and credible ways of measuring success and failure. It is of course important to be clear what the objectives of communication are before engaging in research. Too many people spend time and resources measuring things that make them feel better rather than measuring the contribution communication makes to the business.

Keeping a company well understood and well thought of can only make a positive contribution to its share price performance. A company's reputation also helps determine what a company can do: acquisitions, disposals, mergers and share issues. All major changes, whether of strategy, management, or simply style, become more acceptable or even possible because of the market's confidence in a company. In particular, this means confidence in its management and in its financial strength. It is in these areas that much of the hard work of financial public relations and its achievements are concentrated.

Making introductions

If we take the example of a business joining a stock market, good financial public relations is essential to a company's ability to float and to cope with the intense public scrutiny of its activity and, in particular, of those who manage the business.

Alongside this, financial public relations has a role to play when a company does not achieve its objectives. Whether perceived failure is due to external factors, a need for more time, failure to manage expectations, or simply getting it wrong, a clear explanation of what is to be done to put the situation right is a far better response than hiding behind closed doors and refusing to talk.

Managing expectations is clearly vital in avoiding the perception of failure. However, the rules and regulations surrounding the dissemination of information about a publicly quoted company have made the whole area of managing expectations a public relations minefield.

What are the rules that govern financial PR?

Like all really worthwhile activities, financial public relations should be a careful combination of the stylishly strategic and the timely tactical, and as such should fit in comfortably with every other area of public relations activity. The real difference between financial public relations and its sibling sectors is the rules and regulations that govern it. While there are many areas of activity in which there are rules, it is difficult to think of any where there are so many rules and regulations about what can be said, when, to whom and for what purpose, which are drawn up in some infinite detail, while at the same time leaving so much room for interpretation, argument and misunderstanding.

Take the London Stock Exchange as an example: the anxious frowns of company directors and their financial advisers do not only come from worrying about how to explain their pay increases to shareholders. In recent years, they have also become understandably anxious about what they can say about themselves, and when and to whom they can or should communicate. Changes in the market and reaction to abuses of information have led to the introduction of new rules, regulations and laws that are in danger of clogging the flow of understandable information altogether. Ironically, this is at a time when an improvement in the flow of information from companies is seen as particularly desirable by those that own them.

The pressure on directors and communications people is to give more information at a time when the rules and regulations make it more and more difficult. The communication of financial information can be a high-risk task, and should not be attempted without careful thought and sound professional advice.

It is quite daunting even to list a selection of the key guides and Acts of Parliament:

- The Companies Act;
- The Financial Services Act;
- The Criminal Justice Act;
- The Stock Exchange's Listing Rules;
- The Take-over Code;
- The Stock Exchange's *Guidance on the Dissemination of Price Sensitive Information (Price Sensitivity Guide)*.

Following the succession of massive corporate failures in the USA, new legislation introduced to counter director fraud, known as Sarbanes-Oxley, will have a significant effect on any plc with a US listing of its shares.

For most UK communication advisers the Stock Exchange publications are most relevant. They address directly the problems of issuing sensitive information. They may be self-imposed rules but the cost of transgressing them both in terms of money and damaged reputation can be considerable.

The *Price Sensitivity Guide* is an attempt to deal with the confusion of what information a company should consider as price sensitive. It is of necessity still open to interpretation but the spirit is very clear. It is designed to stop a number of activities that were previously common practice, including selective briefing, particularly of analysts on price sensitive issues, briefing individual shareholders ahead of an announcement and using carefully placed leaks in newspapers to excite or tone down market expectations ahead of results or announcements.

The simple rule is that any price sensitive information should be disseminated through the Stock Exchange to all shareholders at the same time. The problem remains that one person's price sensitive statement is another's confirmation of a well-known piece of public information.

Financial public relations is a specialist business and requires not only a thorough knowledge of all these rules and regulations, but also some experience in how they have been interpreted in the past. The coordination of the issue of information is also crucial if only to stay within the rules. Experienced financial advisers and public relations people are therefore vital.

WHY HAS THIS BUSINESS BECOME SUCH A MAJOR INDUSTRY?

Financial public relations is often wrongly described as a new industry. In fact, it has certainly been around since the days of the South Sea Company, the famous financial 'bubble' that collapsed so spectacularly in 1720, ruining thousands and causing a political crisis. Anyone interested in studying the way that overactive public relations and hype can lose a lot of ordinary people a lot of money should study this 18th-century example that has now entered the language. It is interesting to speculate whether modern 'South Sea Bubbles' such as Enron, WorldCom, Tycho, Polly Peck or Maxwell will still be scandalous and familiar names in 250 years' time.

Corporate communication activity may not be new, but it has changed significantly since the City itself changed dramatically in the mid-1980s. The electronic screen replaced the market floor and small, privately owned firms became absorbed into international banking groups. This process was memorably, but inaccurately, called the 'Big Bang'. The deregulation and opening up of financial markets, which has been happening all around the world, has certainly involved rapid growth in stock markets, not to mention salaries and bonuses. The 'Big Bang' was not the birth of the financial PR industry, but could be described as the beginning of its rapid-growth, 'adolescent' phase.

Financial public relations activity in the City has experienced signficiant growth over the last two decades, not least in the number of financial public relations consultancies: the great figures of City and commerce have always recognized the need to establish a strong corporate image and communicate with the market. Other factors that have contributed to the growth of specialist financial market public relations have included the changing structure and internationalization of trade and industry generally and, in particular, the technological developments that have led to a communication revolution that manifests itself in everything from local cable television to the worldwide information super-highway.

If there is an area that is still being neglected by those claiming to be the experts in financial public relations, it is the growing effect on public relations of the communications revolution. We talk calmly about objectives, messages and audiences at a time when the technology allows ever more subtle and easy ways of delivering customized messages to anyone anywhere in the globe. Whether all this will enhance or dilute the importance of a comment piece in the *Financial Times* is a matter for debate.

The Internet

Like most revolutionary change the Internet has become a mixed blessing for communicators. In many ways it is an ideal communications tool: fast, relatively simple to use, truly global, interactive, selective, colourful and dynamic. However, in the hands of others it can be uncontrollable, misleading, unsourced, unverified and threatening.

So whilst Web sites have rapidly become the main source of information for those wishing to collect information on an organization, its businesses, products, management, policies and practices, many companies have found that other Web sites set up by special interest groups opposed to their activities or mere existence can be powerful sources of false rumour and damaging information. They can result in campaigns building up at a speed that would have been inconceivable even a few years ago.

E-mail has also become the major communications channel for almost any business, but as many recent revelations and scandals have demonstrated, careless e-mails, whilst not perhaps costing lives, can be very damaging and expensive. Yet because a communication is electronic people take less care than when putting things down in black and white.

So fast has the Internet revolution swept through business communication that it is impossible to predict where it will end. It is important to remind ourselves that the same standards of planning, attention to detail and common sense must be applied to this area of communication as to any other.

INVESTOR RELATIONS – IS IT PUBLIC?

All correct-thinking people regard investor relations as a branch of financial public relations, but it too struggles to come up with a decent definition of itself.

At its most basic, it could be described as the direct marketing end of the stocks and shares promotion business. Investor relations centres around the close relationship and two-way communication between the company, its shareholders and those who directly advise them. Those who advise them are principally the stockbroking analysts who were memorably dismissed a few years ago by the then Chancellor, Nigel Lawson, as 'teenage scribblers' – a description that has gone into the language even though many of those 'teenage scribblers' are still around and middle-aged.

Analysts can often be regarded, like journalists, as another conduit of information to the investor audience, although increasingly nowadays, investment institutions have their own in-house 'buy-side' analysts.

As many market traders will tell you, there is no substitute for direct contact with your customers and it is, therefore, extremely important for public companies to maintain a dialogue with their shareholders. For public relations people, this is potentially a very sensitive area. It is particularly important that those facilitating the communication do not get between the company and its owners.

Coordination and consistency

It is also perfectly clear to all correct-thinking people that investor relations has to be integrated totally with corporate and financial media relations. Consistency of message is probably even more important in the specialist area of City public relations than it is in the other areas of communication, not least because of the sensitive nature of so much of the information. There is also a temptation to make life easier by assuming that different audiences are discreet and do not interact.

For example, to those outside the City it sometimes comes as a surprise to find that City journalists talk to City analysts. It should be clearly recognized that to a great extent they live off each other. An analyst with a particular view can supply a journalist with a story, the story can then provide the journalist with a reason to contact a client investor, who then buys or sells the shares which affects the price, giving the journalist another story. Managing this unstable triangle is at the very heart of any financial public relations activity.

A time to speak and a time to remain silent

'Transparency' has become a vastly over-used word in the City but there can be no doubt that the sheer volume of information and data now available at the touch of a button has helped concentrate the minds of everyone in the financial world on just how open and helpful they can be to those who follow and comment upon them.

How open should a company be? Most good communicators would argue for maximum openness and disclosure of information. The many regulators and their rules and requirements make true openness desirable but also difficult and dangerous.

HOW DOES IT FIT IN WITH OTHER AREAS OF PUBLIC RELATIONS?

As already discussed, corporate and financial public relations interlink to the extent of often being indistinguishable. A company's corporate reputation and that of its management are the fundamental foundation upon which financial public relations is built.

In the same way, the quality and reputation of a company's services and products cannot be isolated from its corporate image and the way it is seen by its financial audiences. Financial public relations can, therefore, not be totally separated from the consumer and business-to-business public relations carried out by any company.

The relative strength of a company's corporate brand, and the individual brands of its operating companies and products, depends on the type and strategic approach of a company. However, it is always a dangerous signal to any corporate and financial public relations operator when a subsidiary brand or product's image dominates a company's corporate image among the key financial audiences.

Political and governmental affairs activity also has to be closely coordinated with financial public relations activity. All business and commercial industries are in some way affected by government, whether national, international or local. In addition, the privatization of so many government-owned industries around the world has created a powerful new set of pseudo-government figures known as the regulators. A regulated company's relationship with its regulator is the subject for a book in its own right.

Financial public relations probably differs less across international boundaries than most other branches of the communications industry: financial activity is not particularly affected by cultural differences. The greatest international diversity is in the area of regulation, governmental intervention and state interference. As a result, although many companies are quoted on two or more stock exchanges around the world, every company still has a home base and a home stock market. However, each market has its own rules and regulations, and coordinating the financial public relations activity in different markets is a growing part of the job.

IN-HOUSE OR CONSULTANCY?

There is a healthy obsession among public relations people to debate fruitlessly the relative merits of in-house or consultancy public relations people. Without doubt financial public relations is an area where professional knowledge and skills are needed by even the smallest quoted company in one form or another. The complexity and regulation in financial communication make it particularly important that there is someone around with the knowledge of both the company and the financial markets.

Whether this expertise comes from in-house or consultancy is completely irrelevant. What does matter is the access that the adviser has to the top management of the company and the breadth of understanding they have of the interlinked City audiences of financial media, brokers, banks and securities houses, and share-owning institutions.

It is important to remember that the key description is 'adviser'. It is an even bigger mistake in financial public relations than the rest of the communication industry for the communication experts to get between a company and its audiences. As well as being an adviser we may occasionally be an intermediary but it is important to remember that the message is that of a company and its management, and that 'good' public relations programmes are those that are effective, not those that are noticeable.

CONCLUSION

Getting the right messages to the right people at the right time is still the essence of success. However, it should be pointed out that the greatest public relations strategy in the world can only succeed if the senior management of the company are doing their jobs well and recognize the important role that communications has to play in any public company.

Financial public and corporate relations people, however successful, should keep in mind at all times that they are only part of the communication process. Like comedians who long to play Hamlet, we need to be aware that most of us have a talent to communicate and amuse, but that does not necessarily qualify us to run the whole operation.

A 'good' public relations campaign is one that is effective, not necessarily one that gets noticed. Financial public relations may require more discipline and more technical knowledge than most aspects of communication activity: it also needs to be every bit as creative as the most sophisticated consumer public relations.

FINANCIAL TIMETABLE

Whilst no two companies will be identical in their annual calendar of financial announcement, there is a common pattern for the majority of medium and large companies. If we assume that the company has adopted the calendar year as its financial year then the following outline would be typical:

31 December	Accounts close
February/March	Preliminary results announced followed by a series of investor meetings
March/April	Report and Accounts issued
April/May	Annual General Meeting (including update on trading)
June	Trading statement followed by a series of meetings with investment analysts
July/August	Interim results (half year) followed by a series of investor meetings
November/December	Trading statement followed by a series of meetings with investment analysts

These are the standard announcements made through the Stock Exchange or regulated news service and are the starting guns for a period of frantic press activity. The period after the end of the year or the half year and before the announcement of the results is known as the 'closed period', during which companies must be particularly careful about releasing any significant financial information.

A FLOTATION CHECKLIST

A new company flotation crystallizes the components of a company's financial PR strategy into a short period leading up to a new stock market listing.

● Do you know what the objectives of the campaign are and what the preferred timescale is for achieving these objectives? Do these objectives fit with the long-term strategy of the organization?
● Have you clearly identified the key strengths that are going to be the core of the campaign message?
● Have you identified the weaknesses of the organization and its management, and developed a communications plan for dealing with them when they arise?
● Have you identified who will be the principal spokesperson, ensured that they are properly prepared and media trained, and decided who will support them in presenting the case?

- Is your campaign coordinated with all the other PR and marketing activity being carried out by the organization?
- Have you a clear timetable of events, checked that it fits in with the rest of the company's financial calendar and with all Stock Exchange rules and regulations?
- How are you going to measure your success?

TEN TASKS THAT ARE ESSENTIAL TO GOOD FINANCIAL PR (AND WILL PROBABLY KEEP YOU OUT OF PRISON)

1. Keep control of the flow of financial information and ensure that there is a process in place to make sure all announcements and meetings are properly authorized and approved.
2. Ensure that all communications across different audiences are coordinated and consistent.
3. Learn as much as you can about finance and accounting. Much of it may be jargon, but ignorance leads to error.
4. Become familiar with the requirements of, and the pressures on the various audiences. Journalists, analysts and investors will all respond better if you understand their needs and timetables and seek to accommodate them.
5. Put in place some feedback mechanisms or measurement to gauge your success and/or failure.
6. Be prepared to learn from others. Much of this activity is being done by hundreds of other people: there are lots of good ideas and practices that can be borrowed – build a network.
7. Remember that when the annual report is sent out journalists will only ever look at the page that covers directors' remuneration – so be prepared.
8. Take every opportunity to get across key strategic messages, whether in the standard calendar announcements or when making other announcements such as acquisitions and disposals or changes in senior management.
9. Keep in touch with the key people in your audiences even when there is nothing going on.
10. Don't go drinking with the press office (unless you have a lot of practice)!

5

Business-to-business public relations

Phil Crossley

KEY PRINCIPLES

Business-to-business public relations is all about creating the right communications in the external environment, with controlled messages delivered over a given period to influence key audiences and give the business the best chance of commercial success.

A good business-to-business campaign could include elements from a number of communication disciplines including: marketing, direct marketing, direct mail, event management, advertising, sponsorship and media relations. For most practical purposes business-to-business public relations is any activity aimed at positively influencing a business's key contacts or any organization or individual who may have an influence on these contacts. A public relations campaign may or may not include any or all of the previously mentioned activities, which in the hands of an experienced public relations professional can be combined like a gourmet dish, to create an impact greater than the sum of the parts.

WHERE TO START?

Before embarking on any public relations activity you should ask yourself a few fundamental questions:

- Why are you doing this?
- What are the desired outcomes?
- Which target audiences are important and which are not?
- What are the potential risks?
- What activity are you going to carry out?
- Whose help do you need within the organization to succeed?
- Is the size of the prize worth the effort involved?
- Could the desired outcome be achieved through more direct channels?
- Do you have the appropriate resources and skills to deliver the required results?
- Can you measure the impact you are having effectively?

It is also important to recognize that business-to business public relations is aimed ultimately at improving the commercial performance of an organization. It should not be an activity that exists to satisfy the whims of senior managers or public relations professionals who simply like to be involved in interesting, exciting projects. In organizations that are not run for profit, there can be other legitimate reasons for embarking on organization-to-business public relations, for example in attracting sponsorship from business, or funding for research in the case of a university, or perhaps building loyalty to an organization, or increasing usage in the case of a local library.

In business-to-business public relations both long and short-term commercial objectives can be supported provided the right approach is taken and enough thought is put into planning a logical and creative campaign.

Over the years one of the recurring criticisms of public relations professionals has been the lack of focus on real business needs. With better training and development this is no longer a legitimate observation and greater emphasis than ever before is placed on delivering appropriate results. Public relations however, is not a perfect and totally predictable science. This is what makes it a challenging and enjoyable area to work in.

WHY ARE YOU DOING THIS?

There are many legitimate reasons for embarking on a business-to-business public relations campaign. In every case the starting point should be an understanding of the organization's business strategy. What are its objectives and how will any business-to-business public relations help to achieve this? It is also useful to understand the brand that you are working with. What are the brand values and key strengths of the organization, or in the case of a product, what are its unique selling points?

The requirements of a proactive campaign can be very different from those involved in managing reputation or expectations when bad news is in the offing or when the worst of all disasters has just struck. So understanding the context for the public relations campaign and the external environment is a must. Remember reputation is like a bank: unless the business keeps making deposits it cannot expect to withdraw or negotiate an overdraft when times are bad.

Behind any specific activity is the objective to influence others and establish or build a reputation with an important business sector or individual. The identified audience, sometimes described as 'publics', should have been assessed as having a direct bearing on the current and future success of an organization. Just because an audience may have been important in the past does not mean that they are necessarily important to the future. The target audience will change depending on the issue being tackled and their potential impact on the organization's success.

It is also useful to establish if the activity is targeted at the organizational level, for example to enhance the reputation of an organization within a specific business sector, or to change business customer perceptions of a particular product or service. Ideally activities should be successfully integrated to support both.

Another useful area to review before embarking on any public relations activity is to look at any existing quantitative or qualitative attitudinal research, particularly if the audiences' attitudes have been tracked over time to see how they have changed and what may have influenced them in the past.

Awareness on its own does not guarantee success. This is true of advertising, direct mail, public relations and other forms of promotion. The key is the impact that the communication activity has had on the audience and if it has led to a change in behaviour or attitude, or generated a purchase.

A well-designed attitudinal survey carried out before, during and after a campaign can provide valuable evidence of the campaign's success. However, the audience will also have been influenced by other communications in the general environment. Their attitudes may be changing, without your influence, in a direction that had not been predicted. Armed with this information it is possible to modify activities accordingly over time.

WHAT ARE THE DESIRED OUTCOMES?

It is important to understand and establish your public relations strategy before embarking on any activity. Where are you positioning your organization in the market and against the competition? Define the timeframe in which results need to be delivered, for example if a business is in financial difficulties and needs quick results, it is futile to embark on a protracted public relations campaign. Equally, for a long-established business it may be more important to have high quality, targeted press coverage than to hastily proceed with a media opportunity that may not hit the right tone or audience.

Think carefully about the appropriate key messages that will support the outcomes that are being pursued. At the end of the day people are only human, and ideally messages should cover the business issues but should also try to appeal to the human side of every audience. There is a principle of good customer service, that you should engage a customer in the human dimension of a conversation before leading them into a business discussion. This is a useful approach when dealing with external audiences too. Remember your key messages are your agenda; if they are to strike home you will need to find an angle that will interest the audience. This is particularly true for media relations, where without an appropriate hook you may not achieve coverage and therefore a direct paid-for channel may be a better or the only available route.

It is vital to manage the expectations of the client, employer or management colleagues when embarking on a business-to-business campaign. In my experience, internal conflicts can be avoided if clear campaign success criteria are established by agreement rather than by imposition. Try to avoid accepting targets that are dictated by others; rather, set specific campaign objectives that should be discussed and agreed with key stakeholders. Ensure that an appropriate measurement system is also agreed in advance. It's always better to 'under-promise' and 'over-deliver'. However, don't be surprised if you promise too little and don't get the go-ahead to proceed.

Make sure that all internal stakeholders are informed and involved as much as possible throughout the course of the campaign. They should be briefed regularly on the state of any planned activities. Where possible, any key results and coverage should be highlighted. Be honest if things are not going according to plan, explain why not and what actions will be taken to get the campaign back on track.

Ensure that all relevant staff are appropriately briefed on key messages and are given an outline of what the campaign activity is likely to be before the campaign starts. It is particularly important that any customer-facing call centre staff or sales staff that may come into contact with some of the target audience in the course of their work are thoroughly briefed.

WHO IS TO BE INFLUENCED?

A great deal of effort and resources can be wasted if it is not clear who the target audience is. Within the world population of businesses and business people there is a massive potential audience, so prioritization is vital, as is understanding the segments that are to be contacted. Examples of segmentation include large businesses (plcs or limited companies), small to medium-sized enterprises (SMEs) and sole traders. There are an infinite number of ways to segment business audiences, so this should be considered before starting to plan any communications.

It is doubtful that the resources to target all audiences will always be available. It is also true to say that it is unlikely a perfect match will be achieved between one communications channel and the entire target group. It is therefore important to build a public relations plan that has a mix of activity incorporated into it.

WHAT IS THE PLAN OF ACTION?

For business-to-business there are a number of key channels. The traditional routes of business publications, trade press, business pages of the national and regional papers are always a good area to consider. These can be targeted with business press releases and relationships can be built with key editors and journalists to ensure greater understanding of the business. Whilst free media coverage remains an obvious aim, it may be necessary to recognize that 'paid-for' editorials or advertorials may be the only way forward if the story is not strong enough to be newsworthy or is too commercial. Grand openings of new buildings, facility visits to existing sites, product trials, market research results, key management appointments, financial results announcements, major contract wins or major investment announcements all have the potential to generate successful business trade press coverage.

There are other third-party routes that can be useful as part of an integrated campaign, for example links with business organizations, local Chambers of Commerce of which there are over 60 across the UK, the CBI, or Institute of Directors. There are a number of ways to engage with Chambers of Commerce, such as membership, which can be used to gain access to other organizations and create contact opportunities. As a member it is possible to position a business at events organized by the Chamber either as a sponsor of an event or as a participant. Usually there is a level of activity that will match the objectives and budget. For example, a company wanting to identify exporters in a given area could achieve this through the Chamber as they already have a good understanding of local businesses.

Using local managers as company champions can be an effective way of getting business messages to potential business audiences, but remember that managers' time does not come free of charge and their full cooperation will be needed if this approach is to be successful. Not all managers are up to the task, so it will be necessary to carry out some form of assessment before inviting them to meet the key target audience face-to-face. Inappropriate behaviour or the wrong word at the wrong time can be detrimental to the campaign objectives. Be careful to ensure that managers are fully briefed on key company issues as well as background to the people they are likely to meet. Providing this in a standard format will ensure that they become accustomed to handling the information. This should be given to managers far enough in advance of any event to be useful to them.

Direct mail can form an effective way of communicating a message to the audience. There are many good books on the subject and there is no need to repeat the advice here, except to state that in business-to-business, the principles of effective targeting still apply, so it is important to ensure mailing lists are appropriate, up to date, and any mailing item is fit for purpose. PR practitioners tend to get involved with smaller targeted mailings to key influential audiences, as opposed to direct mailers who will go more directly to the customer base.

Purchasing a copy of the Postal Address File from Royal Mail may be appropriate for organizations carrying out many large volume and varied mailings. However, for most targeted PR campaigns it may be more appropriate to construct a bespoke mailing list from information contained within the business or from other sources.

Do not underestimate the power of the humble letter, but consider the audience. A well-written letter, short and to the point, can have a major impact with key contacts. It may be politically correct to write to the Managing Director of a major business, but if someone else in the company really needs to take action, make sure they are written to directly. Do not rely on senior people passing information down the line; this can be very unreliable and slow to deliver. A manager I once worked for was nicknamed 'Mr Teflon desk' because nothing stuck to it and everyone else got to do the work instantly.

Think carefully about the material that will be sent to the target audience. Many gimmicks have been tried with mixed results in business-to-business and the audience will have seen most of them before. Sometimes a simple approach works; sometimes the multi-pack with a CD-ROM, party poppers or fireworks can have the desired effect. I even once received a pair of 'Jockey shorts' printed with an invitation to a hospitality event at a race meeting. They were in a hand-made box with grass-like material on the outside. A great deal of time had been spent on the mailing. I did not attend the event, but I have not forgotten the company name and the unusual approach did create an impact. A cleverly conceived direct mailing can in itself be used to generate media coverage, thus adding to the overall impact.

Whatever mailing pack is designed, make sure that it reinforces the organization's brand values. Do not be tempted to go for a quick win at the expense of your brand reputation. Grabbing attention with an inappropriate mailing is likely to have a negative effect in the long term.

Newsletters and information sheets can provide a useful low-cost route to important audiences. The frequency and length of these publications is important: too few and the audience will lose the plot; too many and they will not be read. In general it is better in my experience to communicate one key message effectively than to swamp an individual with a mass of information that they may not read. Of course one message may be communicated through several elements, helping to reinforce the overall message and create the desired impact.

Another area to consider is sponsorship. There is a wide range of activities and organizations looking for sponsorship, from pure charitable giving to good causes, to profile-raising sporting events. It is best to think of sponsorship at two levels: social giving, linked to the organization's wish to be seen as a caring company carrying out its social responsibility; and sponsorship activity aimed at building reputation and contacts with key audiences you wish to influence. All organizations should develop a clear policy on 'social giving', with controls in place to monitor spending.

When considering sponsorship think about the synergy with the brand and brand values and what impact the association will have with the sponsored organization. Will this have a positive impact with the key business audiences? The harsh reality is that much charitable sponsorship may generate goodwill with consumer audiences, but may have little impact with specific business customers unless they are somehow emotionally linked to the charity. If sponsorship activities are carried out, ensure that a clear sponsorship agreement is in place, including a pre-planned exit strategy.

Hospitality events can provide good communications opportunities as part of a business-to-business campaign. Hosting tables at business dinners run by the CBI or Chambers of Commerce can be very effective, helping to build good relationships with key audiences. Sporting or cultural hospitality, clay pigeon shooting, the proverbial box at a football ground, a day at the races, tickets to a concert, etc can all be useful in the right circumstances. But be careful: guests can become accustomed to being invited and could expect this as a right in future, leading to potentially difficult situations.

A recent example, which was very successful at combining social goodwill with business-to-business communications, was the sponsorship of a concert at the Harrogate International Music

Festival. Here many key opinion formers in the area had an emotional tie with the event, and the sponsorship provided funds to support the event and improve the amenity value for a large influential audience in the region. By providing a pre-concert drink a selected group of the target audience were collected together for an informal briefing on the business and key messages, which was then followed by a very enjoyable evening's entertainment.

The Internet offers great promise for communications, which many people are trying to exploit to the full. The growth of business-to-business e-mail has been astronomical and the point has been reached where many of us cannot remember what life was like without it. It is the most instant of communication channels: within seconds the well-crafted e-mail you have created can be whizzing through the ether hitting hundreds of key contacts. At the same time your reputation can be enhanced or dashed on the rocks. Once the send button is pressed there is no going back, so check messages carefully and make sure a contact phone number and address details are on the foot of the message. Remember also that once sent, e-mails can be edited or forwarded by others so your control of the message is over once you press send. Beware putting large attachments in e-mails: some can be difficult to open and this can be very frustrating for the person at the other end and can damage reputations.

Be aware of the fatigue factor. A car company has e-mailed me so many times with different offers that I now bin its messages on sight. On the other hand, a public relations company acting for a potential hospitality venue, which they know I am interested in using, e-mailed me to inform me that the venue was to feature on a TV documentary. This is a good example of a piece of targeted and appropriate e-mailed communication that enabled me to obtain more information and also enhanced my view of the public relations company involved.

Businesses are continuing to develop numerous ways of hooking their business contacts through the Web, providing e-mailed product updates, sales details, prices, online invoicing and hotlinks for people to gain more and more information. Is it effective? Only you will know, but be careful to look at more than just hit rates before making a judgement. Think of the Internet as just another channel and measure the actual changes in reputation, not just the amount of activity transacted.

WHAT ARE THE POTENTIAL RISKS?

With most public relations activity there is an identified potential benefit. However, how third parties respond can be totally different to the way it is envisaged and little things can throw plans off course very easily. For example, if a facility visit is organized, transport reliability can have a major impact. If plans have been created with minute-to-minute precision they can be reduced to a complete shambles if a train is late or a bus breaks down. So think about contingencies and build into any plans some degree of flexibility. Spend some time thinking of the negatives or opposites – what messages are not to be communicated to the audience? What would be a bad outcome for the activity? By doing this, potential pitfalls can be identified and contingency plans put in place. If the risks start to grow, consider stopping the planned activity.

WHO ELSE NEEDS TO BE INVOLVED?

In large and complex organizations it is particularly important to ensure public relations activities are understood and supported by marketing, sales functions and human resources. For example, it may be decided that attending county shows with an exhibition stand would be a good activity to carry out to support the company's brand objectives. Support from sales staff to explain products directly with business contacts may be vital if the event is to be a success. Equally, it is important to influence messages used by sales staff in order to reinforce the public relations objectives.

Working seamlessly together is the best way; sadly in many organizations petty infighting and empire-building can get in the way. Communicating what you are doing and sharing plans and objectives with key internal stakeholders are likely to be vital to your success.

WHAT RESOURCES ARE TO BE USED?

Consider this in its broadest sense. Make sure that all the resource elements are in place: finance, people, time, suppliers and organizational commitment. Think about how the plan impacts on other projects. Is it realistic to expect everything to go smoothly? What contingencies are in place? Have you added a safety margin?

Then there's the wonderful world of departmental budget setting. In all organizations financial control is an important element of commercial success. Be honest: does the organization really get a return for investing in this activity? Avoid the historic cost approach – just because x amount was spent last year does not mean you need to spend the same amount this year; you may need more or less to achieve the objectives you have set. Be particularly careful when using external agencies. Whilst most are cautious with clients' money, be aware that amendments, proofs and changes can all swiftly increase costs and need to be planned for.

IS THE SIZE OF THE PRIZE WORTH THE EFFORT INVOLVED?

This can be a tricky question. How can a value be placed on the reputation of the organization or its individual products? Working for a water company at the time of a drought, I found the cost of carrying out briefings to large business customers on water conservation was relatively low. However, their support and impact on that drought situation was potentially massive, so it was a fantastic return on investment. In many other circumstances it is not as clear-cut as this and a sensible judgement needs to be made.

Think about how hard it will be to change the audience's attitude. What do they know already? Are they opposed to everything the organization stands for or are they just against selective issues? Do they support the business, or are they taking a neutral position? Look to deploy different strategies for each group. Maintaining the level of support from key allies/supporters and converting a neutral audience are very different propositions from tackling a hard core of opposition groups.

HAVE YOU CONSIDERED OTHER OPTIONS TO ACHIEVE THE SAME RESULT?

Before embarking on complex public relations activities consider carrying out some desk research. Contact a couple of members of the potential audience to find out what they know about the subject and how they would approach the issue. They may identify an alternative channel which may not have been considered and the planned activity may not be appropriate or have a poor or low impact with the potential audience.

HOW ARE YOU GOING TO MEASURE THE IMPACT OF YOUR ACTIVITY?

Before embarking on any public relations activity it is essential to consider some form of qualitative research to establish the current views of an audience. This can be done through focus groups, followed by more quantitative research, usually done via a questionnaire, during or after the period of activity, to test shifts in attitudes. This can be expensive but for major campaigns can be very informative, helping to focus the campaign at a later date and therefore saving resources that may otherwise be wasted.

Media evaluation can be carried out to cover any sector of the media. This can be very expensive so it is vital that all coverage is tracked against pre-established key campaign messages and that something is done with the media evaluation to tailor future media activity. The traditional measures of the value of media coverage – AVE, the 'advertising value equivalent' of any coverage, or the OTS, 'opportunities to see' – are still the basic ways of scoring media coverage. In recent years OTS has tended to be used more frequently, but neither of these measure impact on the audience, so more direct measurement of audience attitudes as a result of PR activity is advisable.

There are several options to consider when looking at ways of evaluating business-to-business campaigns. These include: at a high level, omnibus surveys of captains of industry run by established research companies; sector surveys again run by established research companies, usually with a marketing emphasis; or bespoke surveys that can be commissioned to monitor attitudes within a defined business audience at a client-specified time and frequency.

SUMMARY

In conclusion, business-to-business public relations offers a massive range of opportunity and potential for successful communications. The best communication activities engage the recipient in an emotional change leading to a clear action: buy product X, consider company Y as a potential supplier, etc. Think before acting: be clear about the desired outcomes and how success will be defined and measured. Don't be afraid to test and try different approaches in different environments; equally what works once will probably work again. Keep your eyes and ears open to see what other people, particularly your competitors, are doing and learn from it. Be creative with the content and design of any communication item or activity, but don't be afraid to stop mad ideas that don't fit the brand values or which create the wrong impact, even if they are the boss's best creative ideas for a fortnight.

Business-to-business campaign checklist

- Clearly define the outcomes you want to achieve and understand how they support the organization's commercial direction.
- Be aware of the timescales in which any activity needs to deliver results.
- Take time to understand the external environment in which you are trying to have an influence and clearly identify the important audiences.
- Review available research, particularly any related to audience attitudes, before you start.
- Consider all forms of communication in the campaign mix before deciding on the final plan, including face-to-face, e-mails, etc.
- Ensure that your key messages are the right ones to have the desired impact.
- Keep key people within your business informed about your plans so they can support you.
- Identify the potential public relations risks of running the campaign and take any appropriate actions you can to limit the potential damage.
- Ensure that you have the right level of financial and people resource to carry out the campaign.
- Establish in advance how the campaign's success is to be measured.

6

Lobbying Westminster and Whitehall

Lionel Zetter

INTRODUCTION

Many individuals and organizations seek to inform and influence government. In a democracy it is their undoubted (but not necessarily undisputed) right to do so.

We are dealing here with lobbying in terms of Westminster and Whitehall. A tremendous amount of lobbying activity is aimed at local government, the Scottish Parliament, the Welsh and Northern Ireland Assemblies, and (increasingly) the European Parliament and the other institutions of the European Union. These areas of activity are, however, outside the scope of this chapter.

WHAT IS LOBBYING?

In recent years the term 'lobbying' has fallen out of favour on both sides of the Atlantic. This follows a number of high profile scandals where firms or individuals (some of them elected representatives) have abused their positions or their access and brought the practice in to disrepute.

Most professionals in the field would now describe themselves as being in public affairs (as opposed to public relations). The area in which they operate is now generally called 'government relation'. What they do, however, is still generally called 'lobbying' – and so this shorthand term is used throughout this chapter.

WHY LOBBY?

There are two over-riding reasons why individuals and organizations seek to inform and influence government: threat and opportunity.

Many organizations that have not previously concerned themselves with the activities of their elected representatives are galvanized by a threat to their livelihood – or their way of life. This threat can originate from Westminster, from Whitehall, or from Brussels – but any remedy usually resides with ministers. The best way to head off a threat is to identify it early. This means keeping a close eye on think-tank reports, party manifestoes, and government consultation documents.

Almost any piece of legislation, primary or secondary, is going to adversely affect somebody. Legislation to make the use of crash helmets compulsory for motorcyclists would, in its original form, have faced Sikhs with the choice of breaking the law of the land or breaking one of their religion's fundamental tenets. The Act that outlawed the possession of handguns following the Dunblane tragedy deprived many gunsmiths of their livelihood and many target-shooters of their hobby. A Bill to ban hunting with hounds would, if enacted, not only deprive many country dwellers of a pastime, but also many huntsmen, blacksmiths and vets of their livelihood. Restrictions on the sale and consumption of cigarettes, whilst saving many lives, would also inevitably cost many jobs in the tobacco manufacturing industry, and also amongst newsagents and tobacconists. It would be naïve to expect individuals, companies and organizations threatened with the curtailment of their incomes not to seek to block (or at least ameliorate the effects of) such legislation.

The basis of the opportunity aspect of government relations is the fact that the government taxes – and spends – a prodigious amount of money. Its budget is now over £400 billion a year, and it spends money at the rate of more than £50 million an hour. Many organizations are understandably keen to get their hands on a share of this pot of gold.

Many charities and pressure groups regard the acquisition of government funding for their members as being a central part of their activities – indeed in some cases it is their *raison d'être*. Whilst the NHS budget is vast, it is finite. It can be the pressure group with the most effective lobby that secures the bigger share of funding. Persuading the Department of Health to ring-fence money for particular forms of illness or treatments can mean that campaigning charities secure a more comfortable existence for their clients. In the process they justify their budgets, and indeed in some cases, their existence.

For many companies – and whole industries – the government is the biggest customer. In the fields of defence and IT, and in the pharmaceutical industry there is no bigger customer than the government. Sometimes it is the company that mounts the most effective lobbying campaign that secures the contract, rather than the company with the best commercial proposal. Where a contract is finely balanced it is nearly always the bidder with the most effective lobbying operation that wins the day.

WHO LOBBIES?

Inevitably it is the big public affairs consultancies that grab the lion's share of the work – and the headlines. Some of these public affairs consultancies are independent, but public relations companies now own the majority. As with most areas of commercial activity, big blue chip companies tend to draw up a pitch-list consisting of the larger consultancies.

Having said that, public affairs is a field where the small company, and even the individual, can thrive. Very little is needed in the way of investment or infrastructure; it is a combination of personal contacts and procedural knowledge which counts in public affairs. Many of the small and medium-sized consultancies have built up a specialization (health, defence, transport) that gives them a valuable niche market that can be immune from the predatory instincts of the big operators. Inevitably, however, specialization restricts the available market, and conflict of interest can be a problem.

Many large organizations prefer to maintain in-house public affairs departments. Some of these handle all of their own government relations work, whilst others choose to also retain external consultancies. Keeping the government relations function in-house enables organizations to build up continuity of contacts with politicians and civil servants, and also helps them to offer a consistent message – and face – to the press and politicians. The kind of large organization that can afford a dedicated in-house government relations team is not restricted to big FTSE 100 companies. Many trade associations and pressure groups regard an in-house public affairs team as being essential to their operations, and an integral part of the service that they provide to their subscribers and members. Whilst charities are forbidden to lobby in the most blatant sense of the word, they can – and do – seek to exert a direct influence on the public policy agenda.

HOW DO YOU LOBBY?

In the mythical golden heyday of lobbying any problem with government could be sorted out with a quiet word in the right ear, or an agreeable lunch. If those days ever did exist, they are long gone.

In the 21st century in public affairs (as in most industries) who you know is much less important than what you know. Even if personal contacts do enable you to open the door to a minister's office, you will find that same minister sitting with a special adviser or civil servant by his or her side, taking notes. That person will be completely unimpressed by the fact that you went to school or university with the minister. He or she will, however, be interested in your argument. How you present your case, how you back it up, and how it stands up to the counter-argument (which they will either already have heard or they will seek to hear) is crucial.

It is a well-known saying that civil servants advise and ministers decide. That is certainly true, but neither ministers nor civil servants (and certainly not special advisers) operate in a vacuum. They are all subject to external pressures and open to a variable extent to external pressures.

So what are the pressure points, and how do you influence decision-makers to decide in your favour?

PRESSURE POINTS

Civil servants

It has already been mentioned that civil servants have a strong influence over the decisions of ministers. In some cases, however, they make decisions themselves. This is especially true in the case of Executive Agencies and Non-departmental Public Bodies. These operate largely independently, although their actions are overseen by the sponsoring Whitehall department and scrutinized by Parliament and either the Audit Commission or the National Audit Office.

The best, and indeed usually the only way to influence a civil servant is through force of argument. The UK home civil service is staffed by dedicated, incorruptible and generally hard-working individuals. They often expect to spend their entire life in the service of the Crown and to retire on an index-linked pension, possibly with a gong. The way to influence them is the way in which they influence each other – through logical, unemotive, carefully prepared briefs that will withstand hostile scrutiny from your opponents. One bit of flawed logic, or one statistic that cannot be substantiated, can ruin the whole brief. If you have a case, and you present it clearly, civil servants will give you a fair hearing. They will then, hopefully, encourage ministers to do the same.

Special advisers

Special advisers have a unique – and crucial – role at the very centre of British public life. In theory these hybrid creatures are civil servants, albeit only for the duration. In practice they are political animals, supportive of the general policies of the party in power, and attuned to the views of the ministers they serve. They provide that minister with advice, write speeches, deal with the media, and insulate the civil service from the potential perils that can flow from straying in to the political arena.

For someone seeking to sound out a minister or arrange an

urgent meeting, a special adviser is often the best first step. They know their ministers' minds, and diaries, and are usually prepared to listen, and to speak honestly – even if it is off the record.

Most senior ministers have special advisers (there is currently a cap of 81 on their numbers), and they have often known them for years. In the past special advisers had a specialist area of interest, and often stayed with departments when their ministers moved. Nowadays they are almost solely the personal appointments of their ministers, and move with them from department to department. They are an essential port of call for anyone looking to inform or influence a minister.

Press and media

As well as listening to their civil servants and special advisers, ministers also pay a great deal of attention to the press. They are inveterate newspaper readers, TV watchers and radio listeners. The opinion of the press undoubtedly influences the way in which ministers think and act. This is true whether it is the national media with their lobby and gallery correspondents, or the specialist correspondents or journals concentrating on the area for which the minister has responsibility.

Ministers often gauge the popularity (or lack of popularity) of a policy by how it plays in the press and media. They also often gauge their own career prospects (or lack of them) by how journalists judge their reputation and standing. If you can get the press and media, or a section of it, to strongly support your case, then you can be reasonably certain that the minister will, first, take notice of and, second, be influenced by the fact. If you can secure a backbench MP or opposition spokesperson some media exposure they will undoubtedly fight all the harder for your cause.

Parliamentarians

The other great influence on ministers is exerted by Parliamentary colleagues – mainly (but not entirely) from their own party. Parliament (both the Chambers and the Committees) is where the pitched battles (or trench warfare) of lobbying often takes place. Company takeover battles, contests for major defence contracts, pro- and anti- camps on moral issues (abortion, euthanasia, hunting) are all slogged out in Parliament.

There is no point in knowing where the pressure points that influence ministers are located if you do not know how to exert pressure on them. Here are some of the tried and tested methods of getting your point across to decision-makers in the political arena. MPs and Peers can be used to influence ministers in a number of ways.

Delegations

Any minister with any sense will agree to receive a delegation headed up by an MP or Peer. Although civil servants (and special advisers) will invariably be present, a case can be put to a minister directly. Having secured the right to visit a minister with a delegation, the trick is to find out precisely how much time has been allocated. Then get the client to make the case – but make sure sufficient time is left for the minister to respond. Otherwise the minister will listen politely for the duration of the meeting, and then thank you for stopping by!

Select committees

There are select committees in both the House of Commons and the House of Lords. In the Commons, select committees shadow Whitehall departments – such as Defence, Home Affairs, Transport and Trade and Industry. Most select committees in the House of Lords are sub-committees of either the European Union Committee or the Science and Technology Committee. They can all send for people and papers (often summoning ministers as witnesses), and the government has to respond to their reports (some of which are debated in the Chamber). Persuading a select committee to hold an inquiry, or giving evidence to one that has been announced, is a powerful way of influencing the public policy agenda.

Parliamentary questions

The fabled 'questions in the House' can be useful. A Written Answer can secure a detailed factual response, whilst an Oral Question gives the asker two opportunities to question a minister, due to the automatic right to ask a supplementary question (which has to be related but does not have to be revealed in advance). The information or assurances secured can then be publicized, and possibly lay the ground for an adjournment debate.

Adjournment debates

Although they take place at the end of the Parliamentary day, adjournment debates are a very useful way of raising issues with ministers and eliciting information from them. There is a ballot every week to secure an adjournment debate, and the Speaker can also then pick one debate from amongst those that have not been successful.

Adjournment debates last for half an hour at the end of the day's sitting, usually 10 pm on a Monday, 7 pm on a Tuesday, Wednesday and Thursday, and 2.30 pm on a Friday (when the Commons is sitting). The normal format is for a backbencher who has been successful to speak for a quarter of an hour, and a minister to then respond for the same period of time. It is usually the most junior minister in the department who is given this task.

Westminster Hall debates

A comparatively recent innovation has been the introduction of debates in Westminster Hall. These take place on a Tuesday and Wednesday, and again backbench MPs enter a ballot in order to secure a debate. There are two debates of an hour and a half each, and three debates of half an hour each. For the longer debates other MPs can participate, as they can at the invitation of the sponsoring member in the shorter debates.

Private Members' Bills

There are a number of different types of Private Members' Bills. Presentation Bills are just that – they are presented to the House, and the long and short titles appear in Hansard, but they make no further progress.

Ten-minute Rule Bills are balloted for and are presented on Tuesdays and Wednesdays, usually at about 12.30 pm. The sponsoring MP can speak and explain why the Bill is necessary, for up to 10 minutes, and another MP can speak against it for an equal period of time. There is sometimes then a vote, but even if this is positive the Bills make no further progress.

There is the annual ballot for Bills at the start of each new session in November. The top 20 MPs in the ballot get help in drafting a Bill, and some Parliamentary time. Only the top three, however, generally have any hope of making it on to the statute book.

All of these Bills help to raise the profile of issues and to concentrate the minds of ministers and civil servants, even if they do not make it on to the statute book.

Government legislation

The government of the day has the sole right to introduce legislation that requires expenditure, and it is generally only government bills that become Acts of Parliament. However, backbench MPs can speak against a government Bill on the floor of the House and in Committee, and even if they do not succeed in securing an amendment, their intervention can sometimes secure assurances from ministers about the intended effects of a Bill, and such interventions certainly do raise the profile of an issue.

No matter how large a government's majority may be it is always possible to change parts of a Bill that are badly drafted or which are likely to have unintended consequences. The best place to do this is in Standing Committee in the Commons, or during the Committee Stage in the Lords (which is almost always taken on the floor of the House). Governments are still vulnerable to time pressures, and occasionally they are even swayed by the force of logical argument.

Early day motions

EDMs are often referred to as 'Parliamentary graffiti'. They enable MPs to place a motion in the Order Paper, and other MPs can sign up to them or amend them. They are never debated, but if an MP refers to an EDM during the weekly debate on the Business of the House the full text is written in to Hansard. Some EDMs deal with trivia such as the success of a football or rugby team. Others, however, deal with serious issues. A rule of thumb is that any EDM that has all-party support or which attracts upwards of a hundred signatures will have an impact.

All-party groups

There are two types of such groups. All-party Country Groups deal with relations with particular countries. All-party Subject Groups deal with a wide range of topics, from (alphabetically) abuse to youth hostelling. As the name implies, such groups have to have officers and members from all the main parties, and these groups also have members from both the Commons and the Lords. Sometimes the secretariat and the funding for such groups is provided by interested extra-Parliamentary bodies. They help to inform MPs, and to keep issues actively in front of Parliament.

Backbench groups

The Parliamentary Labour Party and the Conservatives maintain departmental or policy committees that cover broad policy areas (such as economic affairs, defence, home affairs, foreign affairs or health and social services). In opposition, the officers of these committees are frontbenchers, whilst in government they are back-benchers. They welcome policy papers from expert external sources and they occasionally invite non-members to address them.

Upper waiting gallery

MPs can enter a ballot to hold an exhibition in the upper waiting gallery leading to the committee corridor. They do this on behalf of external bodies that want to raise their profile or the profile of an issue with Parliamentarians and the press. MPs and journalists often congregate in the upper waiting gallery ahead of a committee meeting.

Constituency

The best way to get the attention of an MP – whether he or she is a backbench member or a minister – is through their constituency. They all have to be re-elected every four or five years, and ignoring the interests of their constituents is the best way to ensure that this does not happen. The first port of call for any PA professional is to seek out an MP or group of MPs who have a constituency interest in the issue they are promoting. An alternative is to set up a post-code search on a campaigning Web site and invite supporters and members to find their MP and then approach them directly. Whilst MPs do not generally respond to spam e-mail or untargeted mail-shots, the response rate where the author is a constituent is very high. As former US House of Representatives Speaker Tip O'Neill famously said, 'All politics is local'.

SHOULD LOBBYING BE ALLOWED?

Periodically there are moves in all of the UK legislatures to discuss a partial or total ban on lobbyists. The conclusion has always been that such a ban would be unworkable – and unjustifiable. Legislators are there to be approached, and lobbying is a legitimate and important part of the democratic process.

Lobbyists provide politicians with facts, arguments, and off-the-shelf pre-prepared Bills. This is particularly valuable to opposition parties and backbench MPs, who are faced with a government backed by the Whitehall machine. They also ensure that there is a flow of personnel between the public and private sectors and the fourth and fifth estates. Any attempt to ban lobbying would simply drive it back in to smoke-filled rooms. Given that there are generally people lobbying on both sides of an issue, MPs and ministers end up with a more balanced view than they otherwise would. It is obviously an individual's right in a democracy to lobby his or her MP. As with the courts, most people also believe that it is an organization's right to be represented by a professional advocate in order to have their case presented in the clearest and most robust manner possible. For all of these reasons lobbying should not only be allowed, but encouraged.

LOBBYING TOOLS

There are a number of tools you will need to mount a successful lobbying campaign. These are:

- a system for monitoring developments in Westminster and Whitehall;
- a database that will enable you to identify and then communicate with interested ministers, MPs, Peers and civil servants;
- a database for matching politicians to specific locations by postcode;
- a press and media database.

Some of these tools are still available in hard copy (see the bibliography below), but increasingly the best method of obtaining and using them is via the Internet.

CONCLUSION

Public affairs can be viewed as a branch of public relations. It uses the same communications skills to try and exert influence. However, it is a specialized market in so far as the person to be influenced can be just a single minister. That minister will be advised by civil servants. He or she will also be influenced by Parliament and by the press. That is where the public relations skills come in. Using MPs and the media, a public affairs campaign can shape the climate to the point where ministers are prepared to ignore the advice of civil servants. The ground rules for public affairs are the same as the ground rules for public relations: identify your target audience, prepare your case, and then present the case to the target in the most effective manner possible.

Lobbying is both legitimate and laudable. The practice has been around for as long as there have been governments. The only difference now is that it is more open, more visible and more regulated. MPs and other politicians have taken to complaining about the low turnout at elections. Part of the reason for the low turnout is that the electorate feel that they are divorced from their elected representatives. There are many ways of addressing this democratic dislocation, some of which will take time. But in the meantime politicians should not shut any doors or windows – and they should certainly leave the ones marked 'lobbying' firmly open.

Checklist

Here are some pointers to bear in mind when dealing with Westminster and Whitehall.

SOME DOs

- *Monitor* – Parliament, government departments, political parties and think tanks. That way you won't get caught by surprise.
- *Respond quickly*. Have your response to adverse policies and Bills pre-prepared – both are easier to stop or amend in the early stages before they gather momentum.
- *Identify allies*. It is always better to make friends and allies in advance, rather than have to ask for support before a relationship is established.

- *Use the usual channels.* Try and get what you want by talking to civil servants, special advisers and ministers first, before you resort to involving backbench MPs or opposition spokespersons and the press.
- *Persist.* Often you will not get what you want quickly, and you will have to push your case through the many channels described in this chapter over a long period of time.

SOME DON'Ts

- *Bombard politicians.* Make sure your letters and e-mails are targeted at either constituency MPs or politicians with a genuine interest in your area of operation.
- *Ignore the opposition.* Opposition MPs are often more willing to tackle ministers robustly – and opposition parties do not stay out of government for ever.
- *Forget the press.* The press and other media can be highly influential in support of, or in opposition to a campaign.
- *Drop a politician in it.* Be honest and open with politicians, and never put them in a position where supporting your case is going to cause them embarrassment.
- *Let a minister off the hook.* If you secure a face-to-face meeting with a minister, or one of your supporters secures an adjournment debate, make sure that the minister has time to explain and justify the government's position – and to give assurances if so inclined.

BIBLIOGRAPHY

Politico's Guide to Political Lobbying, Charles Miller, ISBN 1902301250
How Parliament Works, Paul Silk, Pearson, ISBN 0582327458
Erskine May, Parliamentary Practice, Butterworths Tolley, ISBN 0406895872
Guardian Media Guide, Guardian Books, ISBN 1843540142
PMS Parliamentary Companion, PMS Publications, quarterly, ISSN 0965-0415
Vacher's Parliamentary Companion, Vacher Dods, quarterly, ISSN 0958 0328
TSO Political Companion, annual, The Stationery Office, ISBN 0117022705
Civil Service Year Book, The Stationery Office, ISBN 0114301859

7

Local government relations

Beryl Evans and Carl Welham

INTRODUCTION

The days when local authorities had absolute power over public services and governed in a style akin to benevolent dictatorship have long passed.

Today's 21st century council is scrutinized, assessed and inspected on an almost daily basis. The Government has set up a variety of inspectorates to look at specific services. For example there is the Social Services Inspectorate and OFSTED – the Office for Standards in Education. They rate the performance of social services and education and publish the results. It leads to a rating system and a climate in which councils can rate specific services against those of other councils.

In 2002 the Government went one step further and published a Comprehensive Performance Assessment (CPA) of county, unitary and metropolitan councils. CPAs were carried out on behalf of the Government by the Audit Commission and rated councils as excellent, good, fair, weak or poor. Whether they liked it or not, from now on councils were in a league table.

One of the criteria used to judge councils will be their standing with the public and key partner organizations. It is widely acknowledged that communication plays an important part in perception of a council and therefore in its overall rating. Never before has communication been so much at the centre of what councils do and how they think.

LOCAL GOVERNMENT

Local government is based on a democratic system of representation. Just as MPs represent their constituents in Parliament, so the local population has the opportunity to elect councillors to make decisions on their behalf on those services provided by local authorities.

Local authorities count for about a quarter of all public expenditure in Britain. The public affairs remit, by implication, is huge both for the authorities themselves and for those who will be involved in activities that have an impact on a community served by a local authority.

The role of a councillor is one of local representation both to the local community and, in certain instances, to the government and its ministers. While MPs are salaried, councillors are not. (Some councillors holding major responsibilities such as chairing committees or a council leader receive fixed allowances, however.) While MPs have allowances for secretarial and research support, councillors rarely have similar facilities. And in some instances, councillors hold down a job while juggling their personal time to attend meetings, carry out site visits or undertake surgeries for their constituents. Others will dedicate themselves to being a councillor as a full-time role or perhaps take it up after retirement.

A review of the structure of local government in the late 1990s increased the number of unitary authorities, especially in the cities. Despite this there are still several layers of local government:

- metropolitan authorities;
- unitary councils;
- county councils;
- district councils;
- parish and town councils.

In areas where there is a county council a 'two-tier' system exists with the county providing the major services which are best organized on a large scale (such as schools, social services, strategic planning and economic development) and the district council responsible for services such as refuse collection, local leisure facilities and collection of council tax. Elsewhere in metropolitan and unitary authorities, one council provides all the services.

However, just because the council is the provider does not mean that it employs all the staff. Increasingly councils are entering into contracts with private companies to deliver front-line and backroom services. There are arrangements with other public bodies such as the health service to deliver community care.

Parish and town councils do not exist in every part of the country, but where they do, they concentrate on very local matters, and in certain circumstances can act as partners or agents for other local authorities.

HOW COUNCILS COMMUNICATE

Councils are trying to communicate a complex variety of messages. They are primarily trying to publicize their services and show these are good value for money or, if performing poorly, what is being done to improve things. They are also charged with consulting public and partner organizations about the delivery of services and on the future direction of the council and the area. This has led to the creation of a communications consultation industry with surveys, sampling and focus groups abounding. Good councils use this information as a basis for policy development.

Councils have truly come out from the Town Hall. Many have one-stop shops – places where people can call in person or ring for all services under one roof. Some have developed interactive Web sites where people can do anything from paying bills to reporting repairs. Most will have their own newspaper and marketing materials. All will have a press office function to both generate proactive news and deal with enquiries when things go wrong.

The head of communications within the council will usually have responsibility for all the communication channels as well as guiding policy and strategy at both councillor and officer level.

GAINING ACCESS

Though not every authority will have a professional public relations officer with whom to make contact for advice, virtually all will publish their own leaflets or newspapers, take comprehensive entries in the telephone directory, issue citizen's charters and have help points or information centres in public offices such as libraries or service reception areas. Nearly all councils now have their own Web sites. Usually these are constructed from the name of the area with '.gov.uk' added on. For example, the Web site address for Sheffield City Council is www.sheffield.gov.uk.

Such information may be the foundation of effective public sector public relations, but for those who are not familiar with the way councils work it is an invaluable means of identifying what is going on in a community, who the main personalities are and what the local policies are on specific issues.

The lobbying voice for local authorities is the Local Government Association based in Smith Square, London. It lobbies on behalf of councils and represents the sector's voice at national level and with the press. It is also a prime interpreter of policy likely to affect the councils it represents.

When trying to build alliances or determine the strength of the opposition to a project never overlook the views of the appropriate local authority. Elected councillors will want and need to be aware of something that is likely to affect their patch.

Like MPs they will act as a resourceful ally if they share your objectives. They too will want to know about the issues affecting their constituents, given the services that councils provide. Sometimes, via a party political network, or simply through constituency matters, they will be in contact with local MPs to discuss issues of common concern.

Local government is, generally speaking, much more accessible to the public than central government. Council offices and services are situated in the locality, with their committees and the full council meetings – where the decisions are taken – open to the public.

Who writes the committee papers upon which so many hours are spent in public debate? The answer is, the officers – usually. Just as civil servants will advise their political bosses and act in a non-political capacity, so will council officers. Basing their advice on professional expertise and local knowledge, they will offer elected members impartial advice. So they, too, need to be considered an important target for information and potential alliances in public affairs activity.

Be prepared to be referred to a less senior officer, even if your personal approach or letter is made to the chief officer. Many authorities now have 'directorates' with a multi-disciplined person to head a multi-function department; the second or third tier official below that person is most likely to be the individual actually dealing with the matter with which you are concerned.

With major policy matters, usually the appropriate service chief officer or even the chief executive personally takes the lead, in conjunction with leading elected members. Groupings of local authorities are formed on areas of concern – from airport developments to economic strategies – and can be a powerful voice on the national scene, thus making them influential allies or opponents.

PARTNERSHIP

'Partnership' is a word you will hear a lot when dealing with councils. Although they have lost some of their statutory powers and services they deliver directly, councils still exert enormous influence over the shape, rate of growth and character of the area they govern. Services are now often delivered in a 'joined-up way' with partners from both the public and private sectors. Front-line services are often contracted out to a private company to deliver, with the council playing the part of client.

On its own this presents a big challenge to council communicators. They have to wrestle with communicating with their own staff but also with staff who work for contractors delivering services on behalf of the council. It can be confusing for the public when their bins are emptied by a private firm – 'Just who is doing what?' they ask.

However, partnerships have been a good thing for councils. The ones that have adopted a partnership approach have found that their influence and reputation have only been enhanced. New areas of influence have opened up and new alliances forged.

CASE STUDIES

The nature of democracy means local authorities can simultaneously work with or oppose central government. The two spheres of government are closely inter-linked and are likely to remain so, as long as local government funding relies on the central exchequer so heavily and the implementation of government policy implies a key role for local government's services.

While the conflicts will continue with such democratic arrangements in place, the strains will manifest themselves on local communities, businesses, consumer groups, the voluntary sector and other interested parties. But it can be used to advantage in campaigning on issues, or when circumstances dictate that alliances need to be formed and coordinated action is important to win over people, councils or governments. The following case studies set some interesting examples.

LONDON BOROUGH OF BRENT – 'NOT ANOTHER DROP'

This is a joint campaign between Brent Council and Brent Police and funded by the Home Office to tackle the high number of black on black shooting incidents in Harlesden.

OBJECTIVES

- To reduce gun crime in the Harlesden area of Brent.
- To work as a partnership in tackling the high number of black on black shooting incidents in Harlesden.

CAMPAIGN OUTLINE AND IMPLEMENTATION

The strategy for the two-year campaign, which began in January 2001, included the following:

- Focus groups.
- Branding – a slogan, 'Not Another Drop', and a logo, a red drop of blood, appears on all publicity material. The logo doubled as a badge, widely distributed within the local community, that people could wear to show their support for the campaign.

- Poster campaign – a hard-hitting poster showing a young black man lying in a pool of blood under the words, 'Young, Gifted and Dead'.
- Media coverage – editors and journalists from several key publications and radio stations (including pirate radio) were contacted a few weeks before the launch and fully briefed about the campaign and the role they could play in making it a success. As a result, main target media, local and black press, have given the campaign lots of positive and supportive coverage.
- Information line – an information line was set up through which people could get more information about the campaign as well as order NAD badges.

EVALUATION

- A once-sceptical community is now supportive of the council and police campaign.
- Over 3,000 NAD badges have been distributed and several requests per day are still coming in.
- There has been a significant reduction in the seriousness and number of shooting incidents in Harlesden since the campaign was launched.

LIVERPOOL CITY COUNCIL – 'THE NEW LIVERPOOL'

This is a media campaign to positively promote Liverpool and the City Council as a driving force behind the city's regeneration.

OBJECTIVES

- To target the appropriate media in order to garner the maximum amount of positive coverage for Liverpool.
- To position the City Council as a driving force behind the city's regeneration in everything from education, regeneration and sport, to culture, film and music.

CAMPAIGN OUTLINE AND IMPLEMENTATION

The City Council re-engineered its media operation in November 2000, increasing the number of staff to eight-strong – mainly ex-journalists –

in order to effectively promote the city in the media and manage media relations.

Target audiences for the New Liverpool campaign are local, regional, specialist and national media, the aim being to overturn the prevailing negative stereotypes which audiences outside the city may hold and reposition Liverpool as a premier European city.

Positive news stories were targeted to every type of media, from papers and broadcasters in Liverpool to mainstream national broadsheet and tabloid press, local, regional and national TV and radio, and of course trade and specialist press. Negative stories were managed.

The campaign is being continuously developed, and is being run and evaluated in house. Daily analyses are compiled detailing positive, negative and neutral media coverage in both print and broadcast media. The news centre also provides daily broadcast and print briefings, and a daily newsbrief containing cuttings of all articles relating to Liverpool City Council, and the city in general. The first annual report on the media coverage secured was produced in May and revealed positive results.

EVALUATION

Over the last six months positive City Council media coverage has risen from an average of 171 stories to an average of 270 per month – peaking at 345 in March 2001. Negative stories have remained consistently below 100 per month and neutral ones fairly constant at 165 per month.

Postscript

In June 2003 Liverpool was announced as the European City of Culture for 2008. This was the result of a joint campaign by the City Council and key partners in the arts, business and the public sector. It is testimony to the advances made by the city in terms of its reputation.

THE KEY POINTS

The scope for effective public affairs is widespread in today's communication-led society.

Achieving consensus and that all-important third-party support in a transparent atmosphere will be a major plank in the strategy of any organization concerned with gaining respect in its appropriate marketplace.

Sometimes confrontation is inevitable. The strength of the cause will be measured in difficult circumstances and the organization's values called into question. Is it up to it? The public affairs strategy must be sufficiently robust to withstand such scrutiny and the organization's core philosophy and its personnel will be tested. It is under those circumstances when the investment in time and effort will be rewarded, or will fail, in the eyes of the organization's publics.

Ten dos and don'ts for dealing with councils

1. Do have a look at the Web site before making contact – it will usually list all the key players and say what the council's priorities are.
2. Don't assume that you can buy favours. There are strict rules about accepting gifts and hospitality and overplaying this can cause problems for you and the person you are dealing with.
3. Know the difference between a councillor and an officer. Councillors are sometimes called 'Members' as in Members of the council, and are elected by local people in wards. They are the local equivalent of MPs. Officers are paid employees of the council appointed by councillors to carry out policy and manage the council.
4. Read what the local press say about the council – the local studies section of the general library will have a full set of cuttings.
5. Ask what partner organizations there are delivering policies. There may well be government-backed regeneration or development agencies that you need to know about.
6. Don't go to the director of a department or the leader of the council as the first point of enquiry. They will refer you to someone lower down the food chain. If you need to talk planning – go to the head of planning. If you want to talk about marketing – go to the head of marketing. They will get you meetings with more senior officers or councillors if it's necessary.
7. Do network. Find out which big corporate or civic events are happening and get an invitation.

---

8. The Mayor or Lord Mayor has no political power but can have a lot of influence. Do find out who they are and what charities they support.
9. Do speak to the head of communications about a campaign or piece of lobbying work. They are mines of information and advice and will usually give freely of both if you can persuade them that you have the best interests of the area/local people at heart.
10. Do look at the inspection reports and audit commission CPA reports about the council. It will show you key strengths and opportunities to help the council achieve its goals.

Further information can be obtained from the Local Government Association, Local Government House, Smith Square, London SW1P 3HZ, Tel: 0207 664 3000, Fax: 0207 664 3030, Email: info@lga.gov.uk, Web site: www.lga.gov.uk.

8

Community relations

Alan Smith

INTRODUCTION

Never before has corporate 'reputation' been more important to continued business success. Nor has corporate reputation been more fragile and transparent to an increasingly cynical society. Whilst reputation might be a global aspiration, it is usually founded upon local community and public relations. Sweeping statements these may be, but the importance of looking after an organization's local interests can be as vital as any other corporate management objective.

Whatever the nature of a business and however large or small it may be, its relationship with the communities within which it operates will have a fundamental impact on both its reputation and its ongoing success as a business. This being the case, the establishment, implementation and nurturing of a formal community relations policy should be one of the cornerstones of any responsible company's business plan.

This chapter puts the case for creating a professional community relations strategy and policy, explaining why such a policy is necessary, how it should be formulated, what 'tools' are required to deliver that policy, and identifies the benefits to be had. It should not be forgotten, however, that community relations, although a stand-alone element in the business arsenal of any organization, should be viewed within and alongside other elements that make up the wider issue of corporate social responsibility (CSR) covered elsewhere in this book.

WHY HAS COMMUNITY RELATIONS BECOME SO VITAL?

Such has been the revolution in communications and the media that the need for professional and managed community relations activities has never been more significant and essential. The explosion in the use of mobile telephones, text messages, e-mails and the Internet has given individual citizens an incredible array of global communications at his or her fingertips. Internet technology, 'chatrooms', dedicated lobbying Web sites and access to e-mail databases give individuals immense power and influence that can compete with the communication efforts of the largest conglomerate.

By the same token, the growth of multi-channel digital and satellite television and radio programmes, together with the remarkable leap forward in broadcast technology, has given news a greater immediacy and global reach. The media industry itself, like most industries, has rapidly become global, with single media conglomerates owning television and radio stations, national and local newspapers and other media on a worldwide basis. The slightest incident, no matter how remote or small in the great scheme of things within an organization, can very rapidly accelerate into a major, international issue that can quickly affect the reputation of a business worldwide.

In parallel with these developments, society at large and the political face of the world has changed radically in the last decade. Just as the Soviet Union broke into a plethora of independent republics and since then countries ranging from Czechoslovakia to Yugoslavia have broken down into more ethnically based states, so have many developing countries, originally created by boundaries established in imperial days, begun splitting into smaller, either ethnic or religious states. Domestic politics has seen the rise of devolution, not just in the context of the establishment of the Scottish Parliament and the Welsh and Northern Ireland Assemblies, but also the move to create elected assemblies in the English regions.

Society at large is also now far more conscious of the role and importance of minorities – racial, religious or political. Individual citizens' rights are more clearly legislated for, not only in national politics, but also in European and United Nations human rights forums. Never before has a single citizen had such access to support from law and therefore such influence upon the behaviour of a company or organization.

In contrast to the growing focus of society on local issues and local politics, business itself has increasingly moved in the opposite direction. Mergers, acquisitions, rationalization and the need for 'critical mass' have all led to the growth of vast international and global corporations. Food and retail, transport, banking, property, construction, energy and travel are but a few industries demonstrating the growth of global conglomerates.

With society and individual citizens moving in one direction and business moving in the opposite direction, there has never been greater need for focused local community relations by companies. 'Being global, thinking local' has taken on a great deal more significance than a mere sales slogan today. A company's reputation is increasingly dependent upon how it is perceived by, and how it behaves towards, local communities in which it works. And a company's reputation will determine its ongoing success.

Community relations, therefore, is a vital element of the whole concept of CSR and should be seen as part of a wider package of activities undertaken by an organization. It is also something that should involve every single employee, particularly through a genuine commitment from the top. And any community relations policy has to involve all of a company's suppliers, subcontractors, clients and other partners within the business being delivered.

CREATING A POLICY: COMMITMENT FROM THE TOP

Most companies that have established a professional, business-based corporate communications plan, setting out the full range of public relations activities to support the business, will also have a written community relations policy or at least a commitment from the company to foster and nurture positive community relations within every local environment where it works, operates or serves. This will vary according to the nature of that business and according to how that business affects or interacts with its local communities.

The policy needs to spell out quite clearly why the business depends upon good community relations and how it can impact upon the organization – both positively and negatively. It needs the full, unequivocal commitment of the Chief Executive and the board. It needs to exhort every employee to be part of that commitment and to contribute as a representative of the company amongst the public at large.

The bigger the company or corporation, the more important should be the profile of the community relations programme: as in the old rugby term... 'the bigger they are, the harder they fall'! Perhaps demonstrating this best is the construction and engineering industry, where a business has a real, tangible and highly visible impact on every community within which it is building or constructing. It is an industry that is unique in that it creates the very fabric of the built environment and yet has the biggest physical impact on a society during the process of delivering that fabric. The industry involves investing in, building, maintaining and operating key manifestations of our built environment and society such as roads, bridges, offices, houses, supermarkets, law courts, hospitals, schools, colleges and universities, and places of leisure. Yet the process of creating this causes traffic disruption, noise, dust, vibration and numerous other anti-social impacts, albeit on a temporary basis.

In this context, the two main 'providers' of the built environment are the owners or developers of the new buildings (the investor could be ASDA Stores, owner and end-user; or a property developer that will lease that building to a third party and could involve either an office block, retail park or such like) and the contractors undertaking the construction process itself (main building contractor, civil engineering organization, specialist subcontractors, suppliers, hauliers and others in the full supply chain). Each participant in the many processes that produce our buildings and transport infrastructure (roads, railways, bridges, tunnels, ports and harbours, airports) needs to have a total commitment to community relations surrounding a project. The whole chain in the process is only as strong as the weakest link – one rogue haulier that spills mud all over the road leaving a site will tar the whole team with a negative brush.

Commitment must come from the top. 'From the top' has two meanings. First, in the process the top is represented by the client, the investor in the project, who has to establish clear expectations as to the behaviour and interaction with the community by the main contractor and, in turn, the imposition of those expectations by the main contractor upon its subcontractors and suppliers. Secondly, 'from the top' means at the highest level within each participating company. The Chief Executive and the main board need to be seen to be genuinely committed to community relations best practice and the company needs to be openly transparent in this commitment.

Demonstrating best practice in its community relations policies from the investor or developer side of the property/construction industry are Prudential Property Investment Managers (PruPIM), which claims to be 'the largest property investment manager in the UK' with about £12 billion invested in more than 1,000 properties, and Land Securities plc, claiming to be Britain's largest quoted property investment, development and property services company. Both clearly have a very high profile amongst the communities in which they develop their property portfolios and both are extremely active in providing proactive community relations activities. That commitment manifests itself most openly in their Web sites.

On the home page of the Prudential Web site, 'Social responsibility' appears in the main menu. Under that title the opening statement is: 'PruPIM seeks to play an active role in the communities in which we operate' – a very definite corporate commitment from which there is no escape! It goes on to state that the company is:

> committed to a programme of investment in, and partnership with, external organisations, which demonstrably improve the quality and well being of the communities in which we operate. We aim to build and maintain PruPIM's reputation and enhance our business while providing a source of pride in the company for its employees and a focus for their involvement in the community.

Significantly, whilst stating earlier that community relations is a vital element of the whole CSR programme within an organization, Prudential's commitment to social responsibility is reflected in the appointment of a Director of Corporate Responsibility. Indeed, through its shopping centres, which are the focal point for many communities, Prudential currently operates three active community investment programmes focusing on unemployment in deprived communities, community safety and active citizenship and employee volunteering. It has also just launched an environmental programme with BTCV called Grass Roots, which aims to help local communities near its shopping centres transform redundant land back into community use. Total corporate commitment comes from their statement that 'we believe that what is good for the communities in which we are represented is also good for us'.

The Land Securities Web site demonstrates similar corporate commitment, with 'Property in context' appearing on the main home page menu, under which it addresses the key sub-menu for Corporate Social Responsibility, Education, Regeneration, Health and safety, Environmental objectives and targets, Environmental management, and a Carbon emissions trading scheme. The main introduction to all of these titles is this commitment:

> At Land Securities, as a result of the scale of our operations we have long held the view that many of our properties have an environmental and social impact which extends beyond the physical and financial investment we make in them. This is particularly evident across our shopping centres and our development projects and we work hard to integrate our activities into their local communities.

In a similar industry environment, but representing the contracting and construction element, HBG Construction Ltd, one of the largest construction companies in the UK and part of the global, £5.4 billion turnover Royal BAM Group (Koninklijke BAM Groep nv), recently launched its community relations policy throughout the company. The Chief Executive, by way of introduction to the whole community relations policy document, commits the company to the communities within which it operates with this exhortation to staff:

> As individual citizens, as a company and as a partnership with our clients, subcontractors and suppliers, we at HBG Construction care for the communities and environments within which we live and

work. Our type of business, whether involving new construction or refurbishment, inevitably has some impact upon the environment and people surrounding our works – noise, dust, vibration, traffic disruption and similar inconvenience. This simple document will help us all do our utmost to reduce some of the negative impacts on communities resulting from our construction works and to do our best to mitigate any temporary inconvenience.

…The need for responsible community relations… is aimed at reducing external complaints and distractions that unhappy neighbours can cause you. The investment in a little time for the local community early on will pay long-term dividends in the overall construction process… Respect for people and a commitment to nurture understanding between our neighbours and our staff have to be a major priority in all our construction processes.

Clearly, every company will have different ways of communicating this message, customizing it to address the specific impact its business has on its communities. Nevertheless, it is important to spell out why it is essential to the business and to have that definite, unequivocal support from the top. Likewise, this commitment needs to be visible and transparent, whether in widely circulated documentation, or Web site pages, or both.

RESPONSIBILITIES AND AUDIENCES

Any community relations policy or strategy plan needs to establish clear and specific responsibility for implementing and managing the company's interaction with the public and society at large, wherever it may occur. Any individual presence of an organization, whether it be a single supermarket, a factory, a construction site or a car dealership, needs to establish a single person responsible for community relations. That does not mean to say that it is a full-time post as it could well be the store manager himself, the construction foreman or the car dealership's administration officer. The most important thing is that someone has specific responsibility to make sure that all employees at that place of work behave and act in a manner that fosters good, proactive interaction with customers, neighbours and adjacent businesses.

That responsibility should include liaison with all existing and potential stakeholders, covering the whole supply chain. No matter how good the reputation of your local supermarket, you will not be impressed if every goods vehicle delivering to and from that store uses your small, confined street as the short cut to the nearest motorway. Nor will the good name of the house builder be enhanced by the fact that every vehicle going to and from the site covers adjoining roads in mounds of mud and dust.

Every supplier and subcontractor needs to be aware of the company's community relations commitments and to adhere to the standards expected of that policy. Thus the placing of contracts (and indeed the withdrawal of those contracts) should be dependent upon their commitment to supporting the company's own community relations policies.

The representative of the business should also liaise very closely with all relevant local public services. Police authorities, fire services, environmental health officers and local Citizens Advice Bureaus are vital parts of local society and good relationships need to be fostered with these organizations. Similarly, local Residents' Associations, Parish Councils, Education Authorities, including local schools and colleges, and the like are all major stakeholders in the smooth running of the local community and should be part of the business's communications audience.

Politicians, be they the borough councillors, town councillors, county councillors or Members of Parliament, need to be kept informed of any developments that a business might expect to impact on its neighbours. Often it is the local politicians to whom the disgruntled citizen will first turn in the event of any disruption to normal life. If the business already has regular interaction with those politicians, they will be more sympathetic and supportive in such an event.

Last but not least in the list of local audiences is the media. Those responsible for community relations must have a relationship with the local press in particular, as well as radio and television stations where applicable. Openness and honesty with local journalists will always pay dividends. Usually it will be the company's corporate communications or public relations manager who will have the only direct links with the press. Nevertheless, it should be the responsibility of the local company community relations representative to actively encourage interaction with local journalists and to seek opportunities to promote the business locally, either with photo-opportunities related to charitable activities or other actions significant within the community.

PROCEDURES

Any community relations strategy needs to incorporate procedures that should be undertaken by those made responsible for local community relations. Guidance and procedures need not be definitive rules and regulations as often it is not possible to be prescriptive for every situation. Advice and guidance will encourage greater involvement and activity by those representing the company and at the same time will create consistency of actions and image, wherever the company is operating.

The most important set of procedures concerns the handling of complaints. There should be a complaints procedure established to cover any incidents that may occur locally or for any complaints received from the public. Essentially, all complaints must be recorded and the action taken must be logged and dated for future reference. When a complaint is made, a written response or a telephone follow-up call should be made by the person(s) responsible for community relations. Thereafter, actions depend upon the nature of the complaint, the continuity of the problem and the options available to resolve the problem.

If need be, situations that cannot be resolved quickly on a local basis should be linked to a mechanism or procedure that brings in corporate back-up or assistance where required. Corporate 'alarm bells' have to be available where an incident or an issue threatens to take on wider audiences and ramifications. This could be an issue that sparks a reaction from a trade union, which, very quickly, could escalate to a national problem. The sooner such situations are addressed from the top, the sooner they can be resolved.

Other useful procedures include liaison with the press and media. As discussed above, local media can have a profound impact upon an organization and its reputation well beyond the bounds of its local activities. Media relations have to be managed. Formal procedures will govern the circumstances in which local media involvement is beneficial and will identify opportunities that can be seized upon by the local business operation to enhance the organization's reputation or image. It will also provide a mechanism and approval procedure for generating positive press coverage.

In many businesses, school liaison is an important part of their community relations activities. Here again it is useful for procedures and support to be given from the centre for such activities. It could be a recruitment and education issue that is being pursued in local schools and colleges, or it could be a safety matter if it concerns transport, construction or other business activities that could impact upon children or youths in the community.

COORDINATED GUIDANCE AND PROCEDURES

Inevitably, all procedures and responsibilities are created from the corporate department or officer charged with overall company community relations policies – either a dedicated community relations department or part of the wider public relations or corporate communications set-up. Since every employee has a direct responsibility to represent the company in public by his or her behaviour and actions, it is of vital importance that a central, corporate body coordinates, supports and provides guidance and materials for each employee to undertake this role. This will ensure consistency, continuity, commitment and comprehensive implementation of the corporate community relations strategy.

To demonstrate the type of guidance that is both practical and understandable, we can turn again to Land Securities. Each of Land Securities' developments have clear community relations programmes surrounding the project, extending to the general public, schools, colleges and universities, local businesses and other neighbouring organizations. Significantly, it is extremely concerned that any of the contractors it employs on its development projects adhere to the most strict and pragmatic codes of conduct in how they undertake their activities and interact with the community.

At a major city centre development in Canterbury (Whitefriars), Land Securities produced a small leaflet that was issued to every single person involved in any way with the development, entitled *Whitefriars and the local community... A good neighbour guide for contractors*. This document is a perfect example of a visible commitment to the community for the whole supply chain. Its introduction is as follows:

The Whitefriars developers, Land Securities, are committed to reducing the impact of construction on members of the public living, working and visiting the City.

121

Our aims are to:

- Maintain the highest standards of public safety at all times
- Minimize inconvenience to our neighbours
- Maintain continuity of trading and vehicle routes in the City centre
- Separate construction traffic from the general public and retailers wherever possible
- Keep open pedestrian routes and facilities for as long as possible.

The media and many knowledgeable members of the public are watching the development 24 hours a day. This Guide has been produced to help provide a day-to-day reminder of the key issues that need to be addressed to ensure good relations with our neighbours, visitors and local businesses.

The document exhorts all site-based construction personnel to be polite and considerate to the public at all times. It is then the responsibility of those companies providing the construction services on the site, both main contractors and subcontractors, to instil similar responsibilities upon all their staff.

HBG Construction Ltd has produced *A practical guide to best practice for site based responsible community relations*. This document, which is 'dedicated to looking after the needs of citizens, neighbours and customers…', contains an introduction from the Chief Executive, identifies key responsibilities and roles for employees, gives guidance on a range of actions and materials that can be used to communicate with the local communities, and sets up the basis for complaints procedures that should be adopted. The document is a vital element in disseminating and empowering community relations activities throughout the company wherever it operates.

This document clearly establishes direct responsibility for community relations upon each construction project team:

Every project team involved in a construction project has direct responsibility for fostering excellent community relations amongst its neighbouring residents and businesses. From the start of a project, an individual directly involved in the management of the site must be identified as being specifically responsible for community relations and clearly nominated as such on the site organisation plan.

A growing medium through which companies can communicate their community relations strategy to staff and to provide tools for implementation is the intranet. The intranet can provide similar guidance notes to the document discussed above, but can also provide procedures and templates for local press release production, templates for community newsletters and other helpful advice and services.

RESEARCH

An important part of any community relations strategy is research. This ranges from basic corporate research to identify existing perceptions of a company's reputation – generally and locally within the business constituencies – to very specific research into local issues that may be influenced by the company's operations in the region.

Local newspapers and local authority Web sites are usually the best sources for research into local issues that can have influence on a local business. Attendance at Residents' Associations meetings can be invaluable. If need be, a company can organize its own public meetings by hiring the local village/town hall, library or school hall and by inviting the public to attend via advertisements in local newspapers. Here, the company can explain its activities and involve the local people in their project, gain 'buy-in' and obtain their views, concerns and opposition thoughts. The earlier these issues are identified the quicker they can be addressed.

This type of activity provides vital research upon which to base subsequent newsletters, press releases and other community relations activities. It can also identify opportunities where sponsorship or charitable activities by employees can best be directed for maximum impact.

IMPLEMENTATION: PICK 'N' MIX OF TOOLS TO SUIT

There are many ways to build positive relationships with the local community. There is no definitive list as each business, each industry sector and each project has its own characteristics, its own culture and its own identity. Nevertheless, it is advisable to give options that could be used in the broad implementation strategy. These can include the following.

Sponsorship/charitable activities

Many companies have adopted corporate charities which they support from the centre, either as key stakeholders or by direct cash donations. Others delegate all charitable donations to local causes, or even do both. The business operations in the local environment should be encouraged to support local causes, either as a business or, as in many companies, through their regional 'Sports and Social Clubs'. Targeted sponsorship or charitable giving, ranging from sponsoring a local youth football team's kit to raising money for the local hospital appeal, can often be 'matched' from the corporate body to encourage such activities.

Web site communication

A company's Web site can provide vital links for the local community. Feedback boxes and discussion areas can invite local participation in a company's activities. Complaints procedures can be made available and information can be provided.

Newsletter

The production of regular local newsletters, distributed to local residents and neighbouring businesses and schools, can be extremely useful tools. These can provide an open window into the company, introducing key staff to the community, demonstrating commitment to the community and explaining the company's business and its activities. An informed and regularly updated community will be a far more understanding community. A newsletter can also be used to lead the public to other sources of information – the Web site, the public open evening, etc.

Residents' meeting/open evening

As discussed in the section on research, it can be extremely useful to organize local residents' or neighbourhood businesses meetings. The booking of the local village/town hall, school hall or library as the venue to invite neighbours in to talk to key staff, to understand the business or project concerned and to question staff on events or issues affecting them, can be a very good means of fostering local understanding and trust.

Local media

The local media – both newspapers and radio/television stations – is a vital element within the community relations matrix. Although this is generally controlled from the organization's central public relations or press department, the local operation or business must establish close relationships with the media and identify any opportunities where the company can benefit from local publicity. Reputation often depends upon the quality of relationships with local press.

Schools liaison

Links with local schools, primary or secondary, as well as colleges and universities, are important elements for successful community relations. Support of schools by local businesses always has positive feedback. Whether this takes the form of education, with staff involved in teaching or lecturing on their subjects, or sponsorship of sports events, computers or other involvement, any interaction can be positive. It also helps in the company's ongoing, long-term recruitment activities – the better-known and respected companies usually attract the best applicants for employment.

Local government

Local representatives, ranging from the local Parochial Church Council, the Town Council, Borough Council, or County Council, are all vital audiences for a business. Where possible, they should be included in any communications strategy within the community. Participation in public enquiries, planning and other procedures will help in the profile of the company and will breed familiarity.

Public services

A company and its staff can become involved, both at work and in their private capacities, with local public service schemes, such as police initiatives in fighting crime, local environmental schemes being organized by the council environmental departments, or campaigns undertaken by firefighters to reduce the incidence of fires. Corporate affiliation with such schemes gives direct and tangible support to local society and can only reflect positively on an organization.

MEASUREMENT AND ASSESSMENT

Measurement can be undertaken both at corporate and at local level, as discussed earlier in the section on research. Whichever level is selected, the most basic measurement can simply be related to business performance. If the business is not performing locally, then the chances are there is something wrong with your operations within the community where you are working, in one way or another. At the bottom line, good citizenship reflects a good company. It also makes good business sense as our behaviour and attitudes locally will determine how our local customers and clients view us and our services or products.

Practically speaking, there are many methods of assessing success or failure in community relations beyond basic economics. If your procedures are adhered to and there is an effective complaints procedure set up, with appropriate logging, documentation and filing (see above, in the section on procedures), then it is easy to monitor and gauge success or failure by the incidence of complaints, the gravity of complaints and the volume of complaints registered. This should be the most telling research and needs the greatest attention and responsiveness.

Publicity in terms of column inches is never the best measurement tool. Nevertheless, the volume of press clippings and the nature of the coverage can be an invaluable guide as to how the local community perceives your organization and its local activities. This is generally seen to be qualitative research rather than quantitative.

Feedback to newsletters, response on the Web site feedback facility and views gleaned from public meetings are useful tools in the measurement of the community relations programme. In many circumstances, the use of questionnaires can provide the most useful feedback. Questionnaires can be incorporated in newsletters, can be part of an advertisement within the local newspaper, or part of a sponsorship activity on the local radio station. There are many similar ways of distributing and retrieving opinion surveys to identify strengths and weaknesses.

On a corporate level, staff newspapers will often help obtain views from staff about how they and their company are viewed amongst the public where they operate. Or, going down the more expensive route, regular (and this could be annual rather than more frequent) opinion surveys could be commissioned from one of the many opinion research organizations such as MORI.

CONCLUSION

We have established how important community relations are to any business and to its reputation. Recent political, social and technological changes within society at large, combined with the emergence of the global economy, have given even greater prominence to the need for positive, professional and comprehensive community relations programmes, implemented through managed strategies at all levels of the business. And it should not be forgotten that every single employee is a representative of the organization and his or her behaviour reflects upon the image of the whole corporate body.

Every day the newspapers, radio and television demonstrate how vital CSR is to the success of a business. Community relations is a very large and growing element of CSR. Companies playing lip-service to community relations, without genuine commitment from the top, can expect to be punished in the months and years to come. It is difficult to build a good reputation – and easy to destroy one – amongst a local community.

Within the greatest organizations, single small acts can have enormous impacts upon business. But such 'small acts' can be positive ones: a bunch of flowers to a pensioner inconvenienced by one of your company's delivery vehicles can create enormous goodwill amongst a small community.

Every company must have the vision and the aspiration to be at ease with itself in society. By creating, implementing, monitoring and measuring a professional community relations strategy, any organization can feel at ease with itself and its employees can feel at ease with their employer.

COMMUNITY RELATIONS: SUMMARY OF ISSUES

- Community relations is a key element of any CSR programme.
- A company's relationship with the communities within which it operates will have a fundamental impact on its reputation and business success.
- Corporate reputation is often founded upon its success or failure at community relations.
- Universal access to the Internet, via Web sites or e-mail, has given individual citizens greater power and influence over corporate reputation than ever before.
- A commitment to fostering genuine positive community relations must come from the top of the organization and should be clear, unequivocal and transparent – preferably manifested as a written commitment on the company Web site.
- Guidance and advice on best practice in community relations should be disseminated to all employees, explaining procedures and providing the materials to deliver polite and considerate public relations at local level.
- Good community relations can't just happen – clear policies need to be established, coordinated and implemented at all company sites in a consistent, professional manner.
- Know your community, local issues, pressure groups, politics, prejudices, hopes and fears – what are the local newspapers and radio stations saying?
- Identify sensitive local issues and determine how your organization can influence the situation positively: environment, unemployment, education, ethnic minorities, disabled groups, and local charities.
- Assess how all of your operations impact negatively upon the local environment, community or businesses and identify how these impacts can be eliminated or minimized.
- Establish working relationships with local authorities, politicians, police authorities, environmental health officers, fire services, hospitals.
- Build a regular and trusting relationship with the local newspaper, radio and television journalists.
- Encourage staff to interact with the community, to seek opportunities for closer relationships, to feed back ideas where the company can assist.
- Ensure that there is a clear and easy way the public can contact you and lodge complaints – and make sure there is a workable procedure for dealing with such complaints.

- In an increasingly cynical society, any commitments to community relations must be deliverable, achievable and sustainable – avoid empty words and promises as they will come back to haunt you.
- Engage with local community groups such as Parochial Church Councils, Mothers Unions, Youth Groups, to assess how your activities are affecting the community and how problems can be overcome.
- Communicate your community relations policies to all of your suppliers and subcontractors in the supply chain.
- Identify what local charities there are and which may have empathy with your own local operations, then assess how the company may help, financially or 'in kind'.
- Ask local people for their views on your operations and ask how you can improve.
- Make sure your clients or customers know you care for your communities – it is also an important marketing tool.
- Measure, monitor, assess and improve.
- Share best practice and examples amongst the whole organization.
- Be prepared to apologize, to be humble and to say sorry, but ensure it doesn't happen again.
- Good community relations is good business sense.

9

Public relations in the voluntary sector

Fiona Fountain

It is often said, sometimes by those who should know better, that people only work in the voluntary sector because they can't hack it in the real world. This attitude is prevalent but misinformed.

People in the sector work every bit as hard as their counterparts in commerce and, according to a recent survey for Charity Recruitment, get as little as a quarter of the going commercial rate for the same type of work! Moreover, the sector employs nearly 1 million workers. This is 5 per cent of the workforce and 2 per cent of the population – more than are employed in agriculture!

There are over 188,000 charities in the UK, with a total income of over £26 billion a year – funds that for the most part are applied for the benefit of the sick, the poor and the needy. Increasingly these are essential community services that central government is unwilling or unable to fund. So, anybody still labouring under the misconception that the voluntary sector is run by well-meaning amateurs needs to have an urgent re-think, especially if they are planning a career in charity PR.

WHAT IS A CHARITY?

The simple answer might be any organization that is registered with the Charity Commission. In practice, though, the voluntary sector is much broader because there are many organizations that can't or don't need to register with the Commission, yet have aims that are seen as 'charitable'. This includes industrial and friendly societies, as well as some organizations that people assume are charities yet are not – Amnesty International is probably the best known of these.

Most people have a traditional image of a charity as one that works for the benefit of people or animals in distress. However, there are many other types of organizations that, over the years, have been able to secure charitable status. Typically this includes churches, religious groups, museums, galleries, community groups, some sports associations as well as trusts and foundations that make grants to charities. It also includes, somewhat controversially, public schools, most of which have been given charitable status as a result of the original definition of a charity being applied. This is: any organization that works for 'the relief of financial hardship; the advancement of education; and the advancement of religion together with certain other purposes for the benefit of the community'. This inclusive and very subjective definition has meant that organizations that have qualified for charitable status are very wide ranging in what they do, who they do it to and how they do it.

WHAT DOES PR FOR THESE ORGANIZATIONS INVOLVE?

This is largely determined by what a charity does and there is huge diversity here. Some are very small, perhaps one or two personnel or local charities with a specific aim, sometimes geared to the provision of a service for just one person. Others are extremely large and work all over the world and on behalf of many millions of people. The majority though lie somewhere in between. For ease of classification, though, charities can be divided (arbitrarily) into the following five types: individual; relief; disability; animal and environmental; and campaigning.

1. Individual agencies

Individual agencies are those that work on behalf of a single individual. Typically they revolve around the need to provide a specialist service for an individual who is unable, for a number of reasons, to obtain it. They are often very small indeed, at least when they start out. People who are closely linked with the individual, perhaps as a parent or a partner, usually run such agencies. They tend to be extremely passionate about what they do. Over time and in the unlikely event that there are no other existing charities operating in that field, such small charities can grow beyond their initial mission statement.

An example is the Anthony Nolan Trust. Initially, the sole purpose of this charity (run by Anthony Nolan's mother Shirley) was to find a compatible match for Anthony Nolan, than aged 7 and with a rare bone marrow disease that left his immune system unable to fight infection. This was followed, in 1974, by the establishment of a trust, the aim of which was to create a register of volunteers willing to donate bone marrow in circumstances where a match could not be found within a patient's family. The trust is still very active and adds the names of around 19,000 new volunteers every year. There are currently over 330,000 names on the register.

Such organizations present strong, emotive material with which to develop a public relations strategy. However, all too often these organizations are too small and have too little money to implement anything other than a very localized campaign. For this reason it is unusual to see a public relations officer (PRO) involved in this sort of organization unless there is a personal link or the cause has been lucky in attracting a sizeable start-up grant. However, this type of organization does present an ideal opportunity to volunteer. A person wanting to break into public relations, but who has no experience, could make a significant impact for such a charity and, in so doing, create creditable material for his or her CV. Small organizations like this, though, are unlikely to offer professional public relations support so it is advisable to have some training under your belt.

A word of caution: people involved in individual charities are almost certainly going to be deeply committed. They will quickly see through anyone trying to use them, so unless you feel similarly motivated, don't bother approaching with offers of help.

2. Relief agencies

Relief agencies are those that work to provide humanitarian aid both overseas and here in the UK. Easily recognizable examples would be Oxfam and the British Red Cross. Central to the ability of organizations like this to operate, is the need to raise awareness of the plight of a group of individuals or of an economic or environmental disaster. For example, raising awareness of the problems faced by people in Iraq during the war of 2003 could not, in some ways, have been easier. Media coverage was daily and in-depth and made the task of creating sympathy relatively easy.

It was noticeable, however, that over the same period little was seen of the very real humanitarian crises that still exist in Afghanistan, Southern Africa (Zimbabwe, Malawi and Zambia), India and El Salvador (earthquakes) and Mozambique (floods). PR teams from charities working in these areas face a huge uphill struggle to make people realize that these disasters still need attention. Reflecting our own nature perhaps, media interest is generally short-term and, although many won't like what it says about our society, yesterday's newspaper is only tomorrow's chip wrapper.

Public relations personnel in this climate need to be creative and have an ability to present strong, newsworthy arguments that demand attention even when other stories are dominating the news. They are almost certainly going to be experienced and work as part of a team. The largest international aid agencies often have several teams, some working abroad, and have a structure that goes from the most junior support staff right through to top level management. They will probably also be amongst the best-paid staff in the sector even though salaries will still be significantly lower than similar posts in commerce or industry.

3. Disability agencies

Disability agencies are those that work to provide support for people with an illness or a disability. Curiously, public relations in this field can be very difficult to implement once the 'sufferer' is no longer a child. It stems, probably, from most people's reluctance to really accept that such conditions exist and to shy away from anything that demonstrates the vulnerability of the human condition. The rational part of the human mind *knows* this. However, it seems safer to pretend that 'we' are somehow immune or that it only ever happens to other people. For this reason, many people do not know how to respond to those with a disability or an illness – it simply makes them uncomfortable.

Making the case for media interest, corporate involvement or simply financial support, therefore, is never easy for a PRO. And it is made even harder by the fact there are many other hundreds (if not thousands) of similar charitable organizations clamouring for the same attention.

The British Wireless for the Blind Fund has been providing radios and associated equipment to blind and partially sighted people in need in the UK since 1928. This is an extremely worthwhile cause that makes a huge difference to the lives of some of society's most isolated, vulnerable and, generally, elderly people. Yet few have heard of it. Contrast this with organizations like the NSPCC and Childline. These are virtually household names and, whilst it may be seen as callous to point it out, their increased profile (and of course, revenue) is due in no small part to the fact that the 'cause' has greater 'cute' appeal.

PROs in this field must find a way to differentiate what they have to say from all the other messages coming out of similar organizations. Moreover, money for many of these groups comes from statutory sources and budgets are often particularly tight. Public relations staff have to be prepared to work hard and find ways of balancing emotional appeals with the needs and expectations of the client groups, ie, beneficiaries and local authority funders. There are, of course, exceptions as some disability causes have greater appeal than others. AIDS is still sexy, arthritis isn't.

4. Animal and environmental agencies

Animal and environmental agencies might easily have been categorized in the same group as relief agencies. Indeed, animal-based agencies often have many of the same public relations advantages enjoyed by children's charities. Significant differences do exist, though. Some people appear to be very hard-nosed about supporting human causes, even in the face of the most distressing images of death and suffering. However, present them with an image of a kitten being rescued from a derelict house (RSPCA) or an oil-covered bird being cleaned and they melt. Identifying and using such emotive triggers is therefore vital for PROs in this field.

Of course, the client group isn't exactly vociferous, demanding or likely to write to their MP so some aspects of the job are easier. Supporters, though, can be challenging and unpredictable! For example, it might be expected for an organization called the Royal Society for the Prevention of Cruelty to Animals (and its trustees) to adopt an anti-hunting stance.

However, a senior board member recently resigned when the charity tried to take just such a public stand. It seems she was pro-hunting! Interestingly, the same news report that covered this story went on to say that the RSPCA 'had announced plans to halve the number of its press officers'. So take note – when times are challenging voluntary sector public relations posts are no safer than those in industry or commerce.

5. Campaigning organizations

Campaigning organizations are those that work to change the hearts and minds of people. In a sense, they seek to educate and change perceptions. This is typically a key goal of public relations activity and one area in the voluntary sector where good public relations practitioners are especially valued. Typically, there is a need to reach the general public but more often it is key decision-makers in government, industry and other sectors that are targeted. An ability to see and develop issues in the long term and well-developed people skills are prerequisites for public relations personnel working in this area. Knowledge of how the instruments of government work is also needed, as another key aspect of public relations in this field is political lobbying.

Such agencies tend to be quite small but can have enormous impact. For example, the Burma Campaign UK (BCUK) works for human rights and democracy in Burma. It is only a small organization but its sole reason for existing is public relations. It seeks to inform, educate and raise awareness in the hope that this will bring about change in what it describes as 'one of the most corrupt and brutal regimes in the world'. To do this it has adopted some interesting tactics. Chief amongst these is a Trojan Horse move against British American Tobacco (BAT), which jointly owns a factory in Burma with the country's oppressive regime. BCUK has been levelling criticism at BAT for this very reason and has recently bought a small number of shares in order to gain entry to the company's upcoming AGM. BCUK campaigners plan to take this opportunity to air their grievances and ask awkward questions of the company's shareholders. BCUK has created a powerful public relations message – recently helped by a clumsy attempt by the Conservative MP Kenneth Clarke to jump on the bandwagon. It is alleged that he has recently criticized companies for collaborating with the regime in Burma. Perhaps someone should have reminded him that he is the Deputy Chairman of BAT?

COMMERCIAL LINKS

This chapter has, so far, only looked at public relations in the voluntary sector from the perspective of the charity. However, many commercial organizations develop strong links with charities and community organizations to enhance their 'caring' credentials and, at the same time, promote their business interests. As such, even in commercial organizations, there is a need for skilled public relations practitioners who understand not only *how* the voluntary sector works but also *why* it does what it does. And these skills are very important to some very big companies indeed. Get it wrong and the consequences can be dire.

A recent article in *Third Sector* (a voluntary sector, weekly magazine) stated WWF-UK had announced that it was selling all of its 51,000 shares in BP in protest at the petrochemical giant's 'slipping ethical standards'. If true, this will be a major blow to BP, which has often cited its five-year relationship with the charity as clearly demonstrating its responsibility to the environment. The article stated that the charity had become dismayed by the stance BP had taken in regard to the Arctic National Wildlife Refuge in Alaska and the possibility of drilling in this area. The shares, with a current value of £200,000, are a drop in the ocean of BP's worth, estimated at £120 billion. However, the loss of WWF-UK's stamp of approval has far reaching consequences for a company keen to present its ecological credentials.

Public relations at the local level is every bit as significant. A campaign launched recently by the DIY store, B&Q, is a case in point. The company had approached schools to design name badges to be worn by staff at a new local store. The mayor and mayoress judged the competition entries and the winner won the chance to cut the red tape during the opening of the new store. He also won for his school some playground equipment donated by B&Q. In addition, 100 of the new badges are to be sold in the store on the day of the opening and the proceeds are to go to a local hospice. This story had prominent placement in all the local newspapers and, in addition to publicizing the opening of the new store, B&Q was also able to use the editorial as a recruitment vehicle. Score 10 out of 10 for B&Q's PR team. Well done too, to the hospice PR crew for demonstrating to other companies the value of a good PR link with their cause.

SO, IS PR FOR THE VOLUNTARY SECTOR DIFFERENT?

In broad terms, no: good public relations is good public relations. Much like commercial organizations, charities have a number of different audiences or stakeholders, sometimes with conflicting interests. For them, the need to plan, target, action and assess a public relations and crisis management strategy is every bit as vital. Rumours of mismanagement and shoddy quality control can ruin a company. In the voluntary sector a story about the misuse of donated funds or failure to provide a safe, appropriate service can be just as disastrous. In such circumstances commercial partners will drop a charity like a hot potato. Even when such allegations are proven to be false it is still an uphill struggle to generate interest from future funders (commercial, statutory or individual).

So much for the superficial similarities. However, it comes as no surprise to learn that the devil lies in the detail. Large voluntary sector organizations need public relations structures in place that are every bit as complex and all-encompassing as those in big companies. Indeed, many probably have public relations strategies that are more highly developed than most commercial organizations. Simplistically, many companies seem to exist fairly happily by keeping two groups of stakeholders happy and informed – the shareholders (those who own the company) and the customers (those who use its products or services). It is not unusual for these two groups to have conflicting needs. For charities, though, this potential conflict is more complex. A board of trustees typically runs a charity and in a sense these are the owners. These people control what the charity does, how it spends its money and the new services it develops. The other major stakeholder group is service users. This is self-explanatory but not necessarily easily labelled, as some groups might consist of animals, trees, plants or even the entire environment. And to complicate matters further, there is often a subset of the two. That is, people who are trustees but who are also closely associated on a personal level with the 'cause' of the charity, be this a disability, an illness, a social problem or an environmental issue. Service users – the recipients – may also have conflicting interests to those within the charity whose job it is to raise funds. Fundraisers may want to present images of the recipients that are full of pathos and helplessness in order to attract funding. However, these images may be wholly unacceptable to recipients who, in order to gain society's acceptance and enter the workplace, want to be seen as capable and competent.

Volunteers further complicate this mix. These are people who give their time because they believe in the cause. They may also be recipients and/or funders. What's more they cannot be classified as staff because motivating them requires a great deal more subtlety than a pay cheque.

The final major stakeholder group is funders – those people (individuals, corporate or state) who give money to the charity. The most important factor for this group is that the money given is used for the purpose it was intended and used efficiently. Most of these people want to see as little as possible of that donation being spent on administration. So it becomes very important for a charity not only to spend wisely but also (public relations practitioners take note) to be seen to be doing so, especially by this group.

DOES THE SECTOR CREATE ANY SPECIAL PRESSURES, CHALLENGES OR EVEN PRIVILEGES?

It might be tempting to assume that commercial sector public relations must be easier because it inevitably has larger budgets and more resources to throw at a public relations plan. This may have been true once but, as mentioned earlier, this may not be the case any more. Pressure exists in any activity that sets targets and has a limited budget or resources with which to achieve them. In this regard there is little difference between voluntary and corporate activity. In any case, many of the larger charities probably have public relations budgets as large as those of similarly sized commercial organizations and in some cases the charity public relations budgets will be larger.

On the plus side, public relations plans involving human interest will inevitably be easier to implement than those that involve the promotion of products or services. Even a radio for a blind person has got to be more interesting than the electrical board inside it.

So, is there such a thing as a 'feel good' factor when working in the sector? Certainly, people who give freely of their time and money to help a charitable cause have every right to feel good about themselves. For a professional PRO the reward should come in doing a job well and being paid – be this for a charity or a commercial organization. For some PROs, though, this may not be enough and some may stay in the sector (in the face of lower remuneration and less generous employment terms) because they do feel that they are doing something worthwhile and for the benefit of others.

This leads to a cautionary note. There is a tendency within the sector for some senior executives and particularly trustees to have unreasonable expectations of people who work in or for a charity. They often plead charitable status when asking for discounts and may expect time to be given without financial reward. Indeed, personnel and consultants in the sector can sometimes be expected to go that extra mile simply because they are working for a charity. This is a slippery path and one that can erode objectivity and trust. It can also generate considerable resentment. For this reason, it is advisable to try to set clear boundaries between paid work, volunteering and donations.

Within this limited space it has only been possible to provide an overview of the scope and complexity of public relations in the voluntary sector. Working within this sector can be challenging, difficult and, at times, frustrating. It also often requires an unorthodox approach and a good measure of tact. It's never dull and that is probably what makes it such an interesting area in which to work.

GOLDEN RULES FOR WORKING IN CHARITY PUBLIC RELATIONS

DOS

- Get to know how charities work and network like mad, especially if you have never worked in the sector.
- Set boundaries between work, volunteering and leisure – and be firm. Some people in the sector will expect you to go that extra mile for free.
- Consider your language. Use the term 'disability' rather than 'disabled'. A person can't be disabled (whatever that means); he or she simply has a disability – but remember language changes. 'Handicapped' is now rarely acceptable.
- Remember that the money you are spending in your PR activity has been donated by people who need to be assured that they are getting value and that their funds are being used as they intended.
- Remember that you are unlikely to be as well paid as PROs in the commercial or industrial sectors, so be sure that feeling good about what you are doing is sufficient compensation for this.

DON'TS

- Ever forget the needs, wishes or sensitivities of a charity's beneficiaries. If you alienate this group in your attempts to raise profile or assist fundraising you'll regret it.
- Assume that an 'awareness' day or week will guarantee media interest. You'll need to be a lot more creative than this.
- Expect media (or anyone else for that matter) to feel as strongly about the 'cause' as you or your board of trustees.
- Make the mistake of assuming that 'charity' means 'amateur'. Charities and the way they work are as professional as other sectors and in many cases, may be more so.
- Assume that PR in the charity sector is easier than in other sectors. It is every bit as challenging.

For further information about working in public relations in the voluntary sector you may find it helpful to contact Fifth Estate. This is a special interest group within the Institute of Public Relations (Tel: 020 7253 5151) that supports anyone working with public relations in the not-for-profit sector. It holds regular meetings with top rank speakers from the media and not-for-profit organizations, runs a mentoring scheme and provides a membership directory.

10

Sponsorship

Richard Moore

INTRODUCTION

Each day, 3,000 brand messages are flashed in front of the UK's population. Everything we see and touch has a brand message, from clothing to cleaning products, drink to fast food.

With the proliferation of branding through all manner of goods and services and the sheer volume of branded messages being aired, companies are fighting harder than ever to break through the clutter and reach customers' 'radars'. This, combined with the fact that today's consumers have grown up with branding and are increasingly aware that they are being sold to, makes the marketing executive's role all the more challenging. Customers are learning to ignore, filter or reject branding, thus rendering a company's campaign ineffective. Worse still, brand savvy, slightly anarchistic younger customers are likely to reject brands that overtly preach to them without showing any true substance or value. Brands that omit to clearly demonstrate why they have a place in people's lives are likely to be rejected outright. To avoid filtering or rejection, brands should look to create positive experiences for their customers to make their brand stand out from the crowd. Sponsorship can do this.

In becoming involved in sponsorship, brand owners are buying a right to associate themselves with events, organizations and people in order to achieve a number of strategic objectives, for example enhanced reputation, increased brand awareness and achieving greater market share at the expense of a competitor non-sponsor.

For many brands and advertisers, sponsorship can deliver higher degrees of brand awareness and exposure more quickly than more traditional marketing communications activities, such as advertising. However, sponsorship is not a substitute for advertising and needs to be integrated with all the other brand communication tools and techniques, including public relations.

THE SPONSORSHIP MARKET

The UK sponsorship market has undergone a period of rapid growth in recent years. In 1981 the estimated spend was just £51 million; in 2000 this had grown to £732 million. It is expected that the market will continue to grow in the short to medium range at a rate of 8 per cent per annum, although this growth rate may decline if the UK slips into a recession, as experienced at the beginning of the 1990s.

Examples of the rise in sponsorship spending are seen in football with Vodafone's record-breaking £8 million per annum sponsorship of Manchester United, more than twice the level of the previous Premier League record of £3 million paid by Sega for Arsenal. Similarly, the Sydney Olympics generated $0.5 billion compared with $95 million in 1988, a five-fold increase in revenue generation in just 12 years.

The growth rate can be attributed to a number of things, including the establishment of sponsorship as an essential part of the integrated marketing programme for many image-aware brands, and the huge rise in the number of sponsorship properties available for companies to put their name to. It is now possible to sponsor most things, from Notting Hill Carnival to weather bulletins on television to sports teams/people/events.

Although there are a wide and varied number of sponsorship properties, it is recognized that sponsorship segments into four main categories: sport, art, broadcast/media and community (including social, educational and environmental). A review of the size of each segment is given in Table 10.1, which shows that sport is by far the biggest sector with 56 per cent of the market, whilst broadcast sponsorship is the biggest growth area with a five-fold increase in five years.

Table 10.1   *UK sponsorship market, by sector*

	1992 £m	%	2000 £m	%
Sport	239	68	415	57
Broadcast	35	10	176	24
Arts	58	16	96	13
Community/social/business	21	6	45	6
TOTAL	**353**	**100**	**732**	**100**

SPONSORSHIP TRENDS

A review of the latest sponsorship research supplied by Mintel, IPSOS RSL and IM-Research shows the following main trends in the UK sponsorship market:

1. the rise in broadcast sponsorship;
2. the increase in sponsorship by financial service companies;
3. the limited supply of new sponsorship opportunities;
4. the polarization of the sponsorship market into 'haves' and 'have-nots';
5. the surge in cause-related sponsorship activity.

A brief outline of these trends is documented below.

1. Broadcast sponsorship

The field of broadcast sponsorship is relatively new and, although small in comparison with sport sponsorship, is the fastest growth sector. The first recognized example of television broadcast sponsorship occurred in 1988 with Clerical Medical's sponsorship of the operetta, 'The Mikado', on Channel 4. Since then, there has been a rapid rise in spending in this sector, which now generates over £176 million per annum and includes Cadbury's multi-million pound sponsorship of Coronation Street and Coca-Cola's record-breaking £40 million sponsorship of ITV's Premier League football coverage.

IPSOS RSL, the renowned barometer for sponsorship, says:

> Looking through the new deals in excess of £1 million, ITV remains the leading contributor. New 'Reality TV' shows have attracted large sums with Popstars gathering £2 million and Survivor an estimated £3 million. On Channel 4, Big Brother secured £4 million from BT Cellnet (now O_2), four times the value of the previous deal with Southern Comfort.

- Deregulation and the increased number of commercial radio and television stations has led to a mass of opportunities that provide sponsors with a captive, target market.
- Consumer research asking about this type of sponsorship shows a relatively high level of awareness of various sponsors and relatively little resistance amongst adults to the concept of broadcast/media sponsorship.
- However, awareness is particularly high amongst the C1/C2 socio-economic group and tails off significantly for ABs. One of the criticisms of this type of sponsorship is that it is a one-dimensional medium that simply offers awareness and no great emotional bond or leveraging opportunities.

2. Sponsorships amongst the financial service sector

- Until recently, sponsorship was the preserve of the 'booze and fags' industries but now it is the financial service sector (including insurance) that tops the league for sponsorship contribution by industry sector, representing 19 per cent of non-sports and 16 per cent of sports sponsorship deals.

3. Supply of new opportunities

- Although, as mentioned in the 'Sponsorship market' section, there has been a proliferation in the type and nature of sponsorship opportunities over the past few years, recent research shows that the number of large, new sponsorship opportunities coming onto the marketplace is limited and that the majority of sponsorships are three/four-year deals with options for renewal. Specifically, there are very few top of the range sponsorship opportunities that have not already been sponsored or which are likely to come to the marketplace. Exceptions to this rule include the likes of the Wimbledon Tennis Championships, television news programmes and BBC television. However, the majority of these and similar first-time sponsorship properties are restricted by legislation or other regulatory bodies and are unlikely to be available in the near future.

4. The 'haves' and 'have-nots'

● The UK sponsorship market is polarized with the high fee generating, high profile sponsorships, such as Barclaycard's £48 million sponsorship of the Premier League at one end and local and community sponsorships of various good causes at the other end of the spectrum. Mintel's sponsorship research reports that this polarization is set to continue and that the number of events and properties that once occupied the middle-ground will either benefit from the lack of available supply of the high value properties, or will lose their appeal and struggle to generate the funds required.

5. Surge in cause-related sponsorship activity

Cause-related sponsorship (also known as education sponsorship) is the second highest percentage growth in the sponsorship industry behind broadcast sponsorship. It is defined by Mintel as 'Any activity by which a company with an image, product or service to market, builds a relationship with a cause for mutual benefit.' It was initially big in the USA but has now become a popular form of sponsorship in this country. The reasons that companies become involved in cause-related sponsorship are:

● large market that is well targeted by age (pre-school to university);
● positive view towards company;
● reaches target at impressionable age;

- strengthens community relationships – will enhance corporate profile in the community;
- improves customer loyalty;
- helps ensure high quality candidates are available as potential employees.

A good example of an extremely successful cause-related sponsorship is Walker's Free Books for Schools. Launched in 1999, the promotion reached 80 per cent of the population and provided 6 million free books for school in three years. Thirty-four thousand schools have taken part and over 1 billion tokens have been collected so far. The value of the books given away is £32.5 million and, on average, schools received 175 books each.

Tetley's Tea was also successful with its in-school promotion to capitalize on its official sponsorship of Team GB at the Sydney Olympics. The promotion, Free Sports Stuff for Schools, was designed so that children got involved in the campaign, but were not exploited in any way as it was promoted through major grocers and on a product of which mothers were the chief buyer. It was the largest promotion ever of its kind and contributed £18 million worth of much-needed sports equipment to schools around the UK.

WHY SPONSOR?

Well-run sponsorships can deliver staggering results. For example, MasterCard received an estimated $98 million worth of media value for its $30 million FIFA World Cup sponsorship. This result does not take into account the value of the platform for running promotions, advertising, incentives, hospitality, special events, the 125,000 affinity card issues or the image transfer value of being associated with the event.

Guinness' sponsorship of the Rugby World Cup is an example of another extremely successful sponsorship. Guinness paid £16 million in total for the sponsorship (including broadcast sponsorship and advertising) and integrated its campaign with on and off air advertising, promotions, an off trade and on trade campaign, public relations, signage, Web site activities, special events, stunts, corporate hospitality and internal communications. As a result, in the UK, sales of Guinness increased by 17 per cent while Guinness Draught in cans saw a 16 per cent increase.

Carlsberg-Tetley also had extremely successful results via its sponsorship of rugby. Carlsberg-Tetley realized the importance of fully integrating its sponsorship campaign into the marketing mix and ran major on-pack promotions such as 'Kick for a Million' in conjunction with the sponsorship. The results were phenomenal. In the first season of the sponsorship, national sales of Tetley's Bitter rose by 4 per cent at a time when the market in general saw a decline of 5 per cent; over the duration of the sponsorship, distribution of Tetley's Bitter in the south increased by an average of 9 per cent.

Both Levis and Bacardi in the UK have created brand experiences through music sponsorships and have witnessed resurgence amongst marketing-literate, image-conscious young people. Bacardi made the decision to enter into a music sponsorship when the brand lost relevance amongst young people. Music sponsorship was chosen for its ability to build an emotive bond with its target market. The sponsorship was successful in doing this and as part of the integrated marketing campaign, led to a massive sales increase of Bacardi. Bacardi's sponsorship of music festivals created an experience which young people were able to relate to. Debbie Kelly, Experiential Marketing Controller for Bacardi-Martini said:

> Give people something special. Don't insult people's intelligence by expecting them to engage with your product just because you sponsor a team or an event. You have to add value and demonstrate that you understand their needs.

DEVELOPING A SPONSORSHIP CAMPAIGN

When entering the sponsorship market, companies should approach the task in a similar manner to that of any other part of the marketing mix and should understand how each stage of the sponsorship process impacts on the company/brand.

Specialist public relations and sponsorship consultancy, Capitalize, takes a brand marketing approach to sponsorship and has devised a 'Sponsorship strategy wheel', which highlights the process that must be adopted with brands in the design and implementation of a sponsorship strategy. The wheel, shown in Figure 10.1, is simply a logical plan of action to ensure that a sponsorship meets the given business objectives.

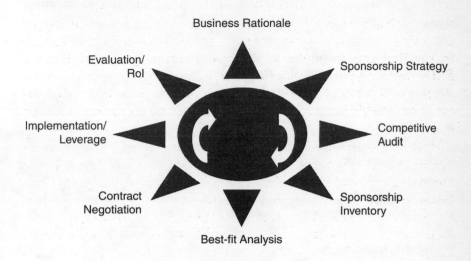

Figure 10.1 *The 'Sponsorship strategy wheel'*

In designing and implementing a full sponsorship strategy, each 'spoke' of the 'Sponsorship strategy wheel' will be considered. These 'spokes' are discussed below.

Business rationale

Before entering into a sponsorship, it is imperative that a company/brand's rationale for doing so is fully understood and objectives clearly set out. For example, objectives may include:

- increasing brand awareness;
- creating a 'feel good' factor within the target market (which must be clearly defined);
- increasing sales;
- generating goodwill amongst employees.

Sponsorship strategy

The sponsorship strategy may differ enormously from one brand to the next brand and whilst, ultimately, most sponsorship initiatives are designed to increase sales, there are a number of different routes to this end goal, including:

- developing customer loyalty;
- growing brand awareness;
- developing new markets;
- internal communications;
- staff motivation;
- staff recruitment;
- launching new products;
- affinity marketing;
- community relations;
- developing product knowledge;
- hospitality;
- good citizenship;
- brand image building.

Competitive audit

When considering entering into a sponsorship, a company/brand should be aware of competitor activity within the area that it is looking to sponsor, so an audit of existing sponsorships should be undertaken.

A competitive audit will ensure that time is not wasted looking into sponsorships that competitors are already involved in. It is also useful when building a sponsorship strategy to know what a company/brand's competitors are doing.

A useful tool in pulling together a competitive audit is IPSOS RSL's Leisurescan and Sportscan, which gives comprehensive information on current sponsorships.

Sponsorship inventory

Once a competitive audit has been made, a full audit of the available sponsorship opportunities should be undertaken. It is usual that during the initial stages of a sponsorship inventory, a number of categories can quickly be dismissed as being inappropriate due to sponsor clutter, competitor activity, international (when national is required), wrong geographical location, etc.

Best-fit analysis

Following the sponsorship inventory and the identification of a shortlist of possible sponsorship opportunities, a best-fit analysis should be undertaken to identify, in detail, the positive and negative elements for each of the shortlisted properties.

The best-fit analysis will demonstrate the potential fit of each property, mapped against the brand requirements. The nature of sponsorship and the process of pairing an organization with the right sponsorship property are somewhat judgmental, so the best-fit analysis is a more structured and organized method of assessing the suitability of each of the properties against a set of objectives.

Table 10.2 shows a sample of part of a best-fit analysis. Other 'subjects' that should be taken into account are target market, sponsorship delivery (eg marketing integration, media coverage), contractual terms, etc.

Table 10.2 *Part of a best-fit analysis*

Subjects	Company's Requirements	Sponsorship Delivery
Brand Profile		
UK Geographical Focus	1. SE England 2. Major Conurbations	London and SE bias
International Spread	None	Televised in 75 countries
Gender Bias	Slight male bias without alienating females	Participation in 60:40 Spectator 50:50
Social Demographics	AB	AB
Age Range	30–45	56% 25–44 years
Brand Essence		
Team-oriented	Team work very important	Social 'team' connotations
Dynamic	Young and dynamic	Young, dynamic
Modernity	Modern approach is complemented with solid performances	Traditional but becoming more modern

Contract negotiation

Once the sponsorship property has been identified, negotiations will commence with the governing body/organization to draw up a contract. Points to look out for when entering into contract negotiations are:

- longevity of contract;
- clawbacks in case of non-delivery of rights;
- indemnity and insurance;
- product exclusivity;
- ambush strategy;
- right to terminate.

Implementation/leverage

Once the appropriate sponsorship opportunity has been picked and contract negotiations initiated, it is prudent to note that in order to achieve the high levels of awareness set in the sponsorship strategy, a detailed campaign will be required, which may include one or all elements of the A-ERIC model shown in Table 10.3.

It was recently reported by IEG that Coca-Cola in America spends upwards of four times the sponsorship rights fee in

Table 10.3 *The A-ERIC model (source: Sponsor Strategi)*

Association	Exposure	Relationships	Integrated communication
Media			
Feeling Values	Television Newspapers The event, etc	The events as a meeting place	Television Radio Print media Internet, etc
Activities			
Positive link Activity	Stadium advertising Kit advertising Opening/closing ceremony Prize giving VIP areas	Invitations Participation Meeting 'celebrities' Kick-off theme VIP areas	Advertising Sales promotion Sampling/sales PR activities Point-of-sale material

leverage. Its research showed the incremental value returned for every dollar spent on leveraging its sponsorship campaigns and that using sponsorship to create Coca-Cola brand experiences was an effective means of generating brand loyalty.

This is an extreme example but is it is worth noting that a budget additional to the rights fee paid for the sponsorship is required to promote a sponsorship to its full potential. The exact level depends on several factors; a rough guideline is given in Table 10.4.

Table 10.4 *Sponsorship budget*

Marketing tool	Percentage of promotional budget in support of sponsorship (%)
Public relations	15–30
Promotions/Incentives	5–10
Hospitality	2–5
Measurement/Evaluation	1–5
Merchandising	1–5
Agency Fees (including legal and accounting)	5–30
Design/Print	2–8
Signage	5–10
Special Events	2–8
Insurance	1–5
TOTAL	39–116

Sponsorship evaluation and return on investment

Sponsorship evaluation and research is key to the management of a sponsorship.

Sponsorship evaluation provides a method that can help to assess the extent to which a company/brand's sponsorship objectives have been achieved. The process of evaluation is one that is extremely controversial and there is still a lack of universally accepted techniques by which sponsorship can be evaluated, that is, by which the value and return on investment can be determined.

That said, certain methods might be put in place to measure the tangible assets, such as media coverage/exposure. Such methods are tailored to each individual sponsorship initiative so that the objectives of the client involved can be assessed. Although not quantifiable, intangible assets such as title sponsorship and public emotion towards a sponsorship should be researched.

Evaluation methods

TV evaluation

Independent evaluation specialists may be used to carry out TV evaluation. This exposure value is determined by the following factors:

- the number of seconds of sponsor exposure taken from the coverage;
- the programme audience (collected from TV audience measurement agencies or alternative best available sources);
- the average peak cost per thousand (CPT) of the country in which the programme was broadcast. CPT figures are used by the advertising industry to establish the advertising cost of reaching 1,000 individuals for 30 seconds. CPTs vary from one TV station to another, from one country to another, and from one year to another.

Media evaluation

Media evaluation may be monitored using independent media monitoring services such as Mediadisk. This provides an equivalent advertising value of a piece of public relations coverage, measuring the page space of the article against a publication rate card.

Research

Sponsorship is designed to build emotional ties with the audience; hence, more in-depth quantitative and qualitative research techniques are required to measure the impact of the sponsorship on individual consumers. Companies/brands should carry out research at the commencement of a sponsorship to create a benchmark from which to assess the effectiveness of the sponsorship. The following areas should be researched:

- spontaneous recall of the brand name;
- type of products/services associated with the brand;

- relevance of sponsor to the event;
- whether the sponsorship has improved the consumer's propensity to purchase the sponsor's goods or services.

The sample researched should match as closely as possible the profile of the target audience in order to obtain the most relevant results for the sponsor.

POTENTIAL PITFALLS TO WATCH OUT FOR

In May 1998, the EU voted in favour of banning all tobacco advertisements (including sponsorships) across EU member countries. Sports have been given until 2006 to find replacement backers. Although major sports such as motor sport, snooker and cricket, which in the past have relied on tobacco sponsorships as a means of income for high profile events, have been hit heavily by this ruling, it is likely that their transition will be a smooth process. Numerous new clients from automotive, IT and finance have approached Formula 1. It is the smaller sports such as fishing, darts and ice hockey that may have a harder battle. It has been suggested in the industry that with the exit of tobacco companies, the cost of packages will fall as it is thought that such companies have been artificially inflating the price of sponsorship in the sports they are involved in.

On 10 January 1991, the *Loi Evin* was introduced in France – legislation restricting the advertising of alcohol in the country. This caused a major stir within the sponsorship arena. It is feared that in the future, the ban on tobacco sponsorship in the EU will spread to affect the producers of beer and spirits.

The impact of European regulators on sponsorship is also a worry and in particular, Europe's desire to break collective bargaining of sports rights by leagues. It is feared that if this were implemented, a great deal of uncertainty to sports rights distribution would be experienced making it hard for sponsors to plan strategically.

A final problem that the sponsorship industry faces is that of polarization, touched on in the 'haves and have-nots' section. The top sponsorship deals are now worth many millions of pounds and therefore only multi-million pound companies can feasibly look to enter into such deals. Deals that are not attractive to blue chip companies obviously do not hold a huge amount of kudos within the industry and therefore smaller companies are less likely to sponsor them. This results in polarization.

SUMMARY

As sponsorship continues to grow with new forms of media, it is important that the fundamentals are not put aside. Although the initial investment into sponsorship buys an association, the need to exploit this further is imperative for a return on investment to be seen. Leverage of sponsorship gains exposure way above any gained solely by contractual rights and it is this, promoting the message that the brand is attempting to communicate, that leads to a successful sponsorship campaign.

The following is a list of dos and don'ts that brands and companies should consider before undertaking a sponsorship campaign:

CHECKLIST

DO

- Set strategic goals that can be tracked during the sponsorship.
- Conduct a full audit of existing sponsorships to ensure awareness of all competitor activity.
- Avoid wastage by ensuring chronological, geographical and demographic fit.
- Apply best-fit analysis to ensure that sponsorship attributes mirror brand values.
- Produce a support marketing campaign to integrate the sponsorship into the brand plan.
- Confirm with the rights holder the extent of its marketing support.
- Seek specialist advice on contract negotiations.
- Implement a dedicated public relations campaign to leverage the sponsorship.
- Allow budget for tracker research so that the effect of the sponsorship on the brand can be monitored.
- Evaluate sponsorship throughout and calculate return on investment.

DON'T

- Consider sponsorship before brand aims and objectives are clear.
- Undertake a sponsorship without reviewing all the options.
- Consider sponsorships in cluttered markets.
- Negotiate a long contract term without vital performance clauses or opt-out clauses.
- Use the entire budget in buying sponsorship rights – ensure sufficient budget remains to promote the sponsorship.
- Pay all the rights fees up front – agree a suitable payment schedule.
- Commence the sponsorship activity without a contract.
- Forget to enjoy it!

11

Communicating corporate responsibility

Martin Le Jeune

A while ago a public relations company asked a range of senior chief executives what single issue or problem was most likely to keep them awake at night. The reply in the vast majority of cases was not commercial pressure, shareholder dissatisfaction, or indeed dealing with restructurings and redundancies. It was hostile press comment.

Putting to one side the obvious question – just how many chief executives have secrets to hide – their answers were revealing and indicate a deeper truth about communicating corporate responsibility: much of it is still driven by personal or organizational fear that unless you have a spotless record, and can point to some form of socially valuable activity, you are a sitting target for a hostile press.

This chapter looks at how accurate and sensible that approach to communicating corporate social responsibility (CSR) is; the part that media relations plays in this area of communications as well as the advantages of direct dialogue; and offers some practical advice for both communications consultants and in-house teams faced with the challenges of promoting good news stories in a suspicious media climate.

A note on terms

The world of corporate responsibility is addicted to jargon and a focus on terminology at the expense of real activity. But a brief word on what we are talking about here should be helpful.

The primary term used here is 'corporate responsibility', which is the umbrella term for a positive relationship between an organization (usually a commercial body, but not necessarily so) and the societies/stakeholder communities in which it operates.

Corporate responsibility is simply a general description. The prime analytical tool used to decide just how positive the corporate-society relationship actually is, is sustainable development. A corporate commitment to sustainable development in essence means that as an organization you put back as much as you take out in any activity, whether it is use of natural resources, human capital, or economic growth. The principle is that future generations should at least enjoy the same access to resources as we do.

'Sustainable development' was not invented by companies (the basic definition was developed by the UN), but it is actually a very useful part of corporate communications, as it puts economic development and wealth-creation as equal partners alongside environmental and social activity. Since so much criticism of the corporate sector starts from the apparent premise that making money is intrinsically wrong, sustainable development can be a welcome route to reminding audiences that no organization that goes out of business can be truly sustainable.

These are the most important terms you will come across. There are others. 'Corporate citizenship' is a rather woolly generic term with the same drawbacks as CSR and roughly the same meaning (or lack of it). 'Corporate community involvement' is in contrast admirably clear – it does what it says on the tin, and if your primary focus is on community work, that is the term that should be used. Communications in this area are covered in Chapter 8 of this book.

THE KEY ISSUE

Communication around corporate responsibility is hampered by one major misunderstanding, so let's clear that up first. However rewarding it may be to develop an employee volunteering system, to paint a hall for the use of a local community group, or to give away a large sum to charity, these have limited potential as far as the national media are concerned. (The picture is rather different on the regional or local stage, of course.) This is because they have little or no hard news value, and it is always worth public relations practitioners remembering the proverbial journalist definition of news: it is something that somebody, somewhere, doesn't want to see in print.

The media focus will always be on key business issues rather than activities which are peripheral to the company, and these are where the media will – rightly – expect to see real corporate responsibility in action: employment and pensions policies; management of the supply-chain; customer service; environmental impact; corporate governance and so on. But these are also subject to the news value test. A company with exemplary employment policies in the Third World is not news; a company which pays its workers starvation wages in poor conditions most certainly is.

Not only are the media disinclined to print heart-warming tales of corporate benevolence, they are also downright suspicious of all corporate activity that claims to be driven by more than sheer short-term profit. Hence the chief executives' fear referred to earlier: it is based on a realistic appraisal of the treatment that they expect to receive at the hands of journalists.

THE PUBLIC RELATIONS RESPONSE

As communication professionals, it sounds as if we should pack up and go home. Far from it. All we need to do is revise the model of communication we are using, and in particular get away from a media relations mindset.

By and large, most senior managers have a simple model in mind when they think of public relations and its effectiveness. It goes something like this:

1. I brief the public relations department with a good news story.
2. The public relations department writes a release and persuades a journalist to write it out – word for word if possible.
3. People read it and think well of me.

Written down like that you can see how unrealistic it all is. And when corporates operate in a climate of suspicion, as today, then it is wholly misleading. The real model for success in communicating corporate responsibility is this:

1. I identify the key stakeholders who are interested in my organization and why.
2. I begin a process of contact and dialogue with them.
3. I respond to their concerns and make my case.
4. They start to be favourably inclined towards my organization.
5. This change in attitude colours what they say to the media, how they react to coverage about my organization, and how the media evaluate my organization and its standing.

Let's look at this process in more detail.

The stakeholder context

There is a lot of fancy footwork over stakeholders, who they are, and what one should do with them. The truth is actually relatively simple.

Stakeholders are the main groups interested in the organization. They are generally obvious enough in broad terms, although every organization has its own specific stakeholder groups:

- shareholders/owners;
- customers;
- suppliers;
- employees;
- competitors;
- 'civil society' (NGOs and pressure groups);
- communities;
- governments and regulators.

In some cases there may be others, but these will do for now.

You will notice that shareholders (or owners/members in the case of organizations which are not companies) come at the top of the list. That is not an accident. Much of current 'stakeholder theory' tries to deny the primacy of those who own the organization, settling for a general statement that all stakeholders are equally important depending on what issue is at stake.

Not only is this contrary to reason, but it also underrates the importance of corporate responsibility as a subject. If it matters, it has to matter as part of long-term organizational success and, in the case of companies, shareholder value. In other words, the more that corporate responsibility matters to an organization, the more commitment there is likely to be. In a business context, if it is not ultimately a shareholder issue, then it is not important.

CORPORATE RESPONSIBILITY IS A BUSINESS ISSUE

Fortunately for communication professionals, corporate responsibility is an increasingly important business issue. So we do have significant material to work with. The reasons are complex but all tend in the same direction.

Corporates operate under much more scrutiny than would have been the case 10 or 20 years ago. This is an aspect of the general decline of trust in institutions – government, the professions, and the civil service have all suffered from it – so corporate responsibility matters in the public and third (charitable) sectors, too.

At least in Western Europe – and corporate responsibility remains very much an area in which Europe leads – there is an implicit distrust of the profit motive and of wealth creation, despite their benefits. That is clearly not going to help business reputation management, but promotes engagement with corporate responsibility.

NGOs are stronger and more numerous, and more professional in their own campaigns. The number of international NGOs has increased substantially in the last decade, and many of them are ready to go on the offensive against companies.

In communications terms NGOs have an in-built advantage: they are more trusted as they are perceived, usually wrongly, as impartial and selfless. What this means is that they are not of course driven by profit, but they compete for resources, media space and reputation as organizations, and that can govern how they promote their long-term goals.

NGOs can have little or no accountability, even to individual members, can be 'flexible' when it comes to the use of statistics and data, and in a minority of cases are ready to break the law in order to further their cause. As commentators have pointed out, this ironically can mean that they are more in line with the hostile portrait of corporate behaviour than the vast majority of companies. In communication terms, though, NGOs start from a high base, and companies from a much lower position. It is relatively easy for NGOs to provide the media with alarmist stories that have a high news value.

However, NGOs are not in fact the most influential movers in the area of corporate responsibility, even if their activities are high profile. It is not just the possibility of hostile external action from NGOs that makes corporate responsibility part of core business management. Anything that has the potential to damage corporate reputation can have a bottom-line impact, so investors themselves are increasingly interested in corporate practice in high-profile areas. The difficulties that Nike and Gap encountered over Third-World clothes and footwear sourcing is one example; BP's bad publicity over its plans in Alaska or its attempt to rebrand as 'Beyond Petroleum' is another.

Investors

The orthodox ethical investor lobby is vocal, but actually rather unimportant in business and financial terms. What is making corporate responsibility more significant is the growth in relatively mainstream investors – people in the UK like the Co-operative Insurance Society or Insight – who see good practice more as part of improving long-term returns than answering some moral imperative (although ethics rather than pure value-generation is a significant background motivational factor in their work).

This growth received an important fillip through a change in UK pensions law that came into force in 2000. It required all occupational and local authority pension funds to state the extent to which social, environmental and ethical considerations were taken into account in the selection, retention and use of investments. Roughly two-thirds of all funds do so to some extent.

The legal change has driven an increase in so-called shareholder/institutional 'active engagement' with companies. Rather than excluding companies that operate in defined sectors (gambling, arms, tobacco, etc) from investment portfolios, active engagement adds the option of maintaining a shareholding and using it to effect positive change in company policies. That may include abstaining or, increasingly, voting against company resolutions at Annual General Meetings. The potential for public and media criticism of company policies as a result is clear.

Combined with the creation of indices that enable investors to select stocks that have fulfilled minimum corporate responsibility criteria – the FTSE4Good and the Dow Jones Sustainability Index are the leading examples – the activities of companies have a higher profile for investors and analysts than ever before. Increasingly the question, 'How did you make your money?', is being asked alongside the more basic 'How much money did you make?' Simple financial questions are being replaced by inquiries that are centred on corporate responsibility.

A CORPORATE RESPONSIBILITY COMMUNICATION TOOLKIT

So far we have established the ground rules for communication in this area:

- corporate responsibility is about real business issues, not peripheral activity;
- media appetite for 'good news' stories is very limited;
- scrutiny of corporate activity is intense and unlikely to diminish.

How do we respond in terms of communication?

Like any good communicator, the first requirement is to find out what's really happening, and challenge the corporate story – whether you are in-house or a consultant. The issues that the organization wants to talk about may not be the issues that its stakeholders are interested in. When did you last read about an NGO campaign that got underway because the employee mentoring scheme wasn't up to scratch?

Stakeholder auditing

A stakeholder audit is the only sensible first step. You can do this as a paper exercise, by talking to people within the organization who have responsibility for various forms of external relations, or by going and talking to people and stakeholders yourself.

In the case of some stakeholders – customers, say, or employees – the sheer numbers may make anything other than quarrying existing data or commissioning new quantitative research impractical. In others, such as competitors or suppliers, you might be lucky enough to have a very small pool to fish in. Circumstances will vary, but the aim of the exercise will always be the same:

- to establish broad stakeholder attitudes to the organization;
- to identify particular issues or concerns;
- to assess overall satisfaction with the way in which the organization is responding to those concerns;
- to develop a communication programme to manage what you have found.

Dialogue

There is a lot more lip-service paid to 'stakeholder dialogue' than actual dialogue taking place. But it is not an exaggeration to say that if you get this part of communication right, everything else is relatively easy; get it wrong, and progress will be extremely difficult.

The two main factors to consider – once you have a definition of stakeholders and some ideas of their views and expectations – are how do we reach them, and how do we generate genuine dialogue? The best way of understanding this is through a real-life example.

CASE STUDY

SHELL INTERNATIONAL: PROTECTING A GLOBAL REPUTATION

Shell is one of the world's largest businesses, operating in over 145 countries and employing 91,000 people. Like most major companies,

Shell has had to move quickly to respond to the rapid changes in stake-holders' expectations of multinationals, evident in recent years as the extent of a business' social and environmental responsibilities is being questioned.

Shell's stakeholders are a diverse and influential group, including the financial community, NGOs, academics, media, government and corporate peers. In 1998, research undertaken by MORI revealed a 'knowledge gap' in their understanding of Shell's policies and principles. Negative views persisted because of a lack of information, and the only way to close that gap was to begin a process of dialogue.

The response was a campaign to open up the company to a series of conversations with its stakeholders, however critical they had been. Significantly, the programme was entitled 'Listening and Responding' and integrated an advertising campaign focusing on issues of climate change, human rights and other dilemmas, with a direct stakeholder communication drive.

The global two-way engagement programme aims to help Shell defend its brand reputation, generate understanding about its business principles and promote a more accurate and positive image about the Group amongst these stakeholders around the world.

The programme takes an integrated approach to communication but is public relations-led: all activity is about creating a dialogue. The advertising is itself used as a public relations tool to lay out Shell's position and solicit responses about Shell's approach, either directly or via Tell Shell, the online uncensored forum launched in 1999.

During the course of the programme, understanding of Shell's business principles has risen dramatically amongst global special publics (opinion formers). In 2002, research revealed that more than 40 per cent recalled an element of the integrated 'Listening and Responding' campaign and research proved that their favourability towards Shell and understanding of its approach to environmental responsibility and social investment had increased dramatically.

A word of warning

Both the Shell Web site – which has won widespread praise for its tolerant approach to all forms of criticisms of Shell, however virulent – and a series of opportunities for Shell people to meet and discuss issues with stakeholders in their own countries, reveal a truth which companies still find difficult: this sort of programme is not about telling the world how wonderful you are, though that may be part of it. It is also about hearing some tough things that people have to say to you.

What is generally true of public relations – you can't make a communication silk purse out of a corporate sow's ear – is absolutely fundamental to corporate responsibility communication. Dialogue presupposes a willingness not merely to listen, but to respond and to change. In the case of Shell, the communication programme would have been a failure had it not been accompanied by a detailed managerial engagement with sustainable development, which had primarily an internal focus. That means that communications professionals need to have the status and internal management structures to put corporate responsibility on the organizational agenda at a high level. Outside audiences will expect that dialogue is at least supported by, and preferably includes, senior management.

Report, report, report

There is a large range of possible ways of handling stakeholder engagement, and the process should not be so complex or time-intensive that neither the organization nor the stakeholders find engagement off-putting. Among the possible elements are:

- a programme of meetings with stakeholders on an annual cycle;
- special events or seminars to address key issues;
- an interactive Web site enabling dialogue;
- membership of organizations active in the corporate responsibility field such as, in the UK, the Institute of Business Ethics, The Institute of Social and Ethical Accountability, or Business in the Community;
- partnerships with NGOs and think tanks to share knowledge and promote the corporate responsibility debate;
- public statements of corporate policy and practice.

This brings us on to one of the most important aspects of corporate responsibility communication: reporting.

Corporate reporting is an issue in its own right as a result of well-publicized accounting scandals. But corporate responsibility reporting was already an issue and a growth area before these developments, because stakeholders want to know more, about more subjects, than the standard format of an Annual Report can provide. The growth in shareholder activism, referred to above, creates the same effect – faced with an ever-increasing number of demands for corporate responsibility information, companies find it easier to collect information and publish it themselves, than to respond on an ad hoc basis. The same applies to organizations of all types and sizes, whether they are commercial companies or not, but for the sake of brevity we will concentrate on the corporate reporting area, most of which applies to non-profit-making bodies.

Reporting might seem a dry subject, but it is in fact critical to the work of communications people in corporate responsibility. Without a report, the suspicion that the organization has something to hide is difficult to refute or shake off.

Changes to corporate governance have also contributed. Following a review, the London Stock Exchange Corporate Code requires companies to include in Annual Reports the arrangements they have in place to manage significant non-financial risk. Examples of significant risks may include – and usually do – those relating to health, safety, the environment, reputation and business probity issues.

There is also current work on producing a new Companies Bill in the UK that seems likely to be more demanding on companies in terms of reporting their corporate responsibility records on the environment, employees and corporate governance.

What sort of report?

There are lots of reports that touch on corporate responsibility issues, ranging from lavishly illustrated community reports which are little more than promotional brochures, to heavyweight documents with more data than the average reader could ever want, backed up by complex Web sites with even more in-depth information.

Which is right for your organization? What are the ground rules? There are useful tips in the Institute of Public Relations guidelines on non-financial reporting, written with the public relations professional in mind, but here are some basics.

The report is not written for the organization itself (although the internal audience may be important in its own right). So one way – the best way – to decide what sort of report, with what sort of information, is required, is to ask your stakeholders what matters to them and report on it.

This will almost certainly lead you down the road of a report that covers a wide range of issues, some economic, some social and some environmental. In other words, it leads you to reporting on the organization's performance against a template, which is very similar to managing and measuring your commitment to sustainable development. As noted above, that is likely to be useful to companies as it balances their obligations to society with their wealth-creation role.

There is no standard format for reports, and no absolute reason why you should adopt one. On the other hand, reporting to some accepted standard makes your report comparable with others and gives it additional credibility. The most promising external standard currently available is the Global Reporting Initiative, promoted by a range of NGOs and others, but with corporate and governmental involvement. In the UK, Business in the Community has launched a corporate responsibility index initiative, although both the bureaucratic nature of the process and the league table aspect have been criticized. There is also a standard on stakeholder engagement promoted by the Institute of Social and Ethical Accountability (AA 1000).

The other advantage to using an external standard is that it empowers communications people to press for information from within the organization. That may sometimes be the most difficult part of the whole process.

So much for the basics. Perhaps the most important issue once the process of collecting data and reporting has begun, is whether to have the information formally audited or at least verified by a third party. The major accountancy firms offer this service, as do smaller organizations that offer 'CSR/social auditing'.

Going down this road is very much a judgement call. There is a cost implication, but also the benefits of enhanced credibility, especially with NGOs. The key questions to ask are, what standard the auditors are using, and what is their previous experience.

MEDIA RELATIONS AND CORPORATE RESPONSIBILITY

So far we have hardly touched on corporate responsibility and media relations, partly because there is very little dedicated reporting in this area. The *Financial Times* and, to a lesser extent, the *Guardian* are the only mainstream newspapers that regularly cover corporate responsibility issues, with a markedly more critical tone in the latter.

There is also a small but thriving corporate responsibility 'trade press', including the long-established *Ethical Performance,* and the newer, more magazine-format, *Ethical Corporation.* These are useful for picking up tips and keeping abreast of sector developments, but the danger of preaching only to the converted is obvious.

The picture is not quite as bleak as this sounds. As corporate responsibility becomes a more mainstream issue, it can be picked up by the business press, including specialist titles covering management, auditing, risk management and corporate governance. If you have initiatives or news that are of particular interest to a business function or sector you should consider seeking coverage in these titles.

The same applies to sector-specific publications. It is difficult to think of a sector that does not have corporate responsibility issues of particular relevance or salience. These are likely to be covered in their trade press. By analogy, coverage in local and regional newspapers relevant to your organization is a form of dialogue with local communities that are important to you.

Communicating via the media is not unimportant provided it is seen as a specific part of a wider stakeholder dialogue. The capacity of the media to oversimplify or sensationalize issues is something that all public relations people have to cope with. One of the ways of ensuring that the impact of negative publicity is limited, is to create a climate in which it is seen by stakeholder audiences who already have enough depth of knowledge about your organization to put coverage in context. It will still affect them, but ideally they should feel empowered to approach you directly to get the true picture, rather than assume that the worst is true.

REACHING CONSUMERS

Can corporate responsibility communication play any role in a consumer-facing organization? Opinions differ.

Some point to successful initiatives like Tesco's 'Computers for Schools' or Walker's similar programme for books. But these are strictly speaking marketing initiatives, although whether that matters to consumers is doubtful.

There has been much less done in the way of using core corporate responsibility values to reach consumers. The famous examples – the Body Shop, the Co-operative Bank, Ben and Jerry's – are famous because they are unusual, not typical. Although individually different, they have non-business values or origins that enable them to stand out from the vast majority of companies. It is difficult to imagine a large, well-established corporation with a typical shareholder base being able to reinvent itself in that way. And who would believe it anyway?

Most research seems to show that only a small minority of consumers take corporate responsibility considerations *systematically* into account when making purchasing decisions, although many more do so occasionally. There are signs that a market is emerging in advising companies on how to use sustainability and corporate responsibility policies and practices in advertising and marketing, whereas most public relations activity in this area has concentrated on communication with opinion-formers. But a little judicious scepticism about whether this really pays off is still justified.

CONCLUSION

Any communications practitioner who gets involved in corporate responsibility is stepping into an exciting landscape that seems to change virtually daily. Effective communication on corporate responsibility involves the ability to manage complex programmes of stakeholder dialogue, achieve internal change, handle the media sensitively, understand public affairs, and fire-fight when things go wrong.

However quickly the land shifts, though, there is one constant. Corporate responsibility is now a major business issue, and having some grasp of it is essential to a good communicator.

TEN THINGS TO REMEMBER

1. Manage internal expectations of results – good news is not news and it's a suspicious world out there.
2. Don't get hung up on the media – stakeholder dialogue may not be visible but it pays off.
3. Outside audiences are interested in every aspect of the way your organization is run; so should you be.

---

4. If you don't report and don't engage with criticism you are storing up long-term trouble.
5. Do you know what your major stakeholders think of you and whether they are happy or unhappy with your performance? If you don't, you are making decisions without any idea of where you are.
6. If you are unable to admit in public where you are at fault, then don't start on corporate responsibility communications.
7. Your internal audience deals in business/organizational issues and must be approached on that basis.
8. Spend time networking and keeping up with developments because corporate responsibility is a moving target.
9. Don't be browbeaten by criticism into panic. Your view of what is responsible may be the right one on a controversial issue.
10. Don't playact at dialogue – raising unfulfilled expectations is worse than not starting.

12

Public relations in the service sector

Tony Langham

What do we mean by service sector public relations? First of all, what do we mean by service companies or brands?

Traditionally, we mean brands that bring a service to customers, such as retail, restaurants, financial services and transport services. To this we can add all forms of consultancy, from management consultants through investment banks to IT and software businesses. In a country where more people work in hotels and restaurants than in all of our manufacturing industries we're talking about a large sector of business life.

Services public relations is becoming easier to identify. Of the 13 'industry sectors' used by *PR Week* in its 2003 Contact Directory League Tables, at least six are for services public relations (hi-tech, financial services, leisure/travel, professional services, retail and media). This is a sign that services public relations – the demand for expertise to advise service brands – is one of the fastest growing areas of the industry. And it's easy to see why, because service brands present three distinct communications challenges:

1. Differentiation is difficult as, whether you offer airline travel, ironed shirts or a rocket and parmesan salad, your competitors

can (and will) claim to offer it just as well, using virtually the same words. If words can be difficult, so too can pictures as you often can't hold or even see the offering.

2. Delivering the 'brand promise' is equally hard. The consistency and control that Disney, BMW and Sony exert over their 'products' is just a dream to the service company brand manager. The service company experience is delivered by the cashier, the hotel maid or the consultancy team 'sent' to Kazakhstan to advise on privatization. This puts emphasis on employee communication and training – and on the handling of customer complaints.

3. History – because of the difficulty in differentiating service brands and in delivering the brand promise, service companies often started later in trying. As a result visual identities and mission and value statements are often less fully developed. Often, communication and marketing functions don't have the status they deserve in service companies.

All of which means that there's nothing more boring than the service company corporate video ('This is our Leeds call centre'). Or the service company 'new product press release' ('New software innovation targets insurers') or listening to a service company talk about themselves ('We are a full service agency'). But then again, there's no more challenging area of public relations.

So while the day-to-day public relations activity for a service company looks much like that described elsewhere in this book under marketing communication, business-to-business public relations, financial public relations and employee communication, the best 'services public relations' draws on nine core themes:

1. As the offering is intangible you need to *prove the benefits* (or prove the need).
2. Words are cheap, so find your *happy customers* and showcase them.
3. Don't say you're the best, find *third-party endorsement*.
4. *Creativity* is vital.
5. As several organizations understand industry issues and can give a considered 'middle of the road' view on the latest development, to succeed you must establish and maintain *thought leadership*.
6. Often, the way to do this is to harness the *intellectual capital* in the firm and make some of it publicly available.

7. The media tend to know something about the area allocated them so *specialist media relations* professionals are vital.
8. If your brand is intangible, it can be assisted by an *association with other brands*.
9. And last, but very often not least, consider making a virtue of the intangibility of 'service' and, on occasion, allow a *sense of mystique* to develop.

1. Prove the benefits (or prove the need)

Where 1970s marketing textbooks would say 'sell the sizzle', the present-day services public relations equivalent would be 'prove the sizzle' – or at least demonstrate the benefits. The problem is that you may not be the best placed organization to prove that your software consultancy really does offer innovative solutions that work and are delivered on time and on budget.

A tried and tested alternative is to approach things from the opposite direction – it may not be possible to prove the benefits, but you can almost certainly prove the need for the service in the first place. In 1992 Lansons Communications was asked how industry body IFA Promotion could better promote Britain's independent financial advisers. The solution, TaxAction, quantifies the massive amount of tax paid unnecessarily each year (usually around £5 billion) through a mixture of inertia and poor financial planning, and offers access to Britain's independent financial advisers as the answer. The campaign ran for it eleventh year in Spring 2003, has attracted over 300,000 requests for advice and is one of the longest running in the service sector. The lesson holds true for so many service industries and companies. It is not possible to prove whether people who take independent financial advice are better off than those that don't – but it's relatively easy to prove that poor financial planning is disadvantaging millions.

In many cases, when challenged to prove the benefits of a service, it pays not to protest too much – and to rely on others to say it for you. Hence the focus on showcasing happy customers and making the most of independent third-party endorsement.

2. Happy customers

'It would make a great story but it needs a case study' says many a journalist to many a services public relations specialist, every working day of the year. 'Case study', as the name suggests, is industry speak for a 'real' person or company interviewed and often photographed about their 'real' experience.

For many service companies case studies provide the only regular, cost-effective way of communicating their service differentiators to their target audience through the media. If you want a journalist to write about how new software developments can increase the efficiency of company supply systems, you need a real company to open its operation to a journalist to 'prove' it. Intangibles like the benefits of advice, or the joy of rail travel (don't laugh) are best brought to life by real experience.

The idea is one of the oldest in marketing, of course. Testimonials, often from celebrities, were a staple of 19th-century advertising in the UK and USA. Likewise, in fields like travel and motoring, journalists reduce the need for case studies by 'road testing' things themselves (poor lambs). For real hardship cases – unlikely to come from companies themselves – there is the point of view or letters page.

If the technique is so old and well understood, why spend time discussing it? Two reasons. First, in the Big Brother age, the demand for real people, real experience, human interest is on the increase. The media want to portray their ordinary readers, viewers and listeners across many of their stories. At one extreme this desire has been capitalized on by a succession of award-winning 'reality' public relations campaigns. Perhaps the first and arguably best of these is the RED Consultancy's work for Microsoft in 1999, isolating four volunteers in a London youth hostel for 100 hours, armed only with the Internet, a bathrobe, a PC and a £500 spending limit. As I said, reality public relations, bringing the 'case studies' to life.

The other reason for discussing case studies is that so many service companies cannot provide them. In fact the majority of service companies cannot provide an ordinary customer or Chief Executive of a client who is happy to discuss their positive experience on the record with a journalist and be photographed.

In my view this is simply unacceptable. Of course it is difficult to do: many people don't want to appear in newspapers talking about their personal experience, but it is not impossible. Here are five tips for getting case studies of happy customers:

1. Recognize the amount of time it takes – anything from two to 10 hours per case study, from calling 20 people to get one to agree, to liaising with the journalist over time, place and availability to be photographed with family and children, etc.
2. If the customer interface is personal, you have to work with the salesman or call centre operative to identify case study targets.
3. If the answer is, 'We can't go direct to our customers because we sell through intermediaries' or, 'We can't because our clients are busy Chief Executives of successful companies', adopt a different strategy. Intermediaries and successful companies often want 'free public relations' and many will be more than happy to cooperate if you do all the work and they appear in a desired publication in a favourable light.
4. As the whole exercise is time-consuming you may need to recompense people for their time – either your own staff for helping identify people, or the 'case studies' themselves for their time (a mixture of a framed print of the resulting article and flowers or champagne, are our preferred means).
5. Above all else, entrust the job of finding case studies to the person with a pleasant and sunny manner. You don't want to alienate five customers simply persuading one to take part.

Of Lansons' 60 clients, the vast majority can supply case studies at one time or another, with between 10 and 20 companies geared up to regularly supply them at short, or no, notice. IFA Promotion has worked with Lansons to elevate the provision of case studies to a high art and, through IFA Promotion media services, has 160 independent financial advisers throughout the country networked and ready to supply case studies on demand, at an average of three a week to national newspapers alone. But if you're in public relations and your company or client claims to be unable to supply case studies, adopt the words of the journalist: 'Without a case study it doesn't make it as a story – and anyway, if you can't find a happy customer for me to speak to, why should I believe you?'

3. Third-party endorsement

In our cynical world it is often easier to say, 'Don't just take my word for it, listen to the world's leading independent...'. This is even truer in the intangible world of service. From the Michelin guides, to independent financial advisers, to retail analysts, to a leading professor or psychologist, to *Which?*, the independent expert is often king.

Independent groups can't be controlled or guaranteed of course, but they can be influenced, just like any other audience. A few thoughts on relations with third-party bodies:

- Easiest first: when you get a favourable endorsement make the best use of it that you can. This can involve a degree of subtlety, so you may have to prevent that direct mail shot from going out immediately. Alerting a range of journalists to the endorsement may be the most effective form of action. There's little point offending the independent body as they will probably be providing the same report again in a year's time.
- With regular industry reports or updates, make sure you're familiar with the timetable and, if possible, offer to help with things like discussing criteria, methodology and which issues are prioritized. Most service industries have an annual review or league table or report that acts as a bible to many users.
- If an independent body assesses you unfavourably, talk to them – ask them why, discuss what they said – and if you can discuss future criteria and assessments.
- If you're confident of your own performance in a fair competition, stimulate independent assessment (for example, approach the Consumers Association and suggest they look at an area) or even 'sponsor' the review yourself (albeit the least effective means, unless the independent organization's reputation is significant).

While none of this can change reality, at the margin, treating the independent assessors, commentators and experts as an audience to be communicated with and persuaded can make a significant difference to a company's rating.

4. Creativity

Many services public relations briefs appear unlikely at best – we are launching a (fill in innovative service enhancement misnamed a 'product') aimed primarily at our (distribution network). It is important however that the new 'product' achieves a high profile with our ultimate customers, be they organizations or individuals.

Two things are normally true about such a brief: a) the new

'product' is unlikely to be interesting enough in itself to create the profile with customers and the, mostly, national media that reaches them; and b) the company itself doesn't have the charismatic CEO, brand or budget to offer an easy alternative.

For this reason a high level of creativity – of the appropriate, applied kind – is a must for almost all major services public relations programmes. For services brands, the creative process needs to have some additional elements to it:

- Spend a lot of time understanding things from the customers' point of view. 'What's in it for me?' This is particularly important in the current 'Does what it says on the tin' environment where there is a growing resistance to better mousetraps.
- Sound bite the benefits and prioritize them – they're likely to include saves time, saves money, less hassle, safer – and try to articulate the more difficult hoped-for benefits, particularly the more intangible 'Gives me good reason to believe it will make things better'.
- With simple themes, consider the widest most ambitious solutions – in particular don't be limited by 'media only' thoughts. Make sure you cover the two extremes of macro-economic solutions (what this would mean for the UK as a whole) and the micro of tabloid daily life.
- If national media coverage is the objective, spend time on each of the main areas of 'news page' coverage including:
  - humour, can we make people laugh,
  - politics, is there a 'campaign thought' in there,
  - celebrities, who fits the bill, could be affected, etc,
  - arguments, who could we fight, and should we,
  - bad news, if we weren't doing this what would happen – or who isn't doing this that needs to be exposed?

This should take you miles from where you started – and that could be the right place to be, as many of the services public relations campaigns that have won PR awards show. A good example is one of the public relations decisions taken by Six Counties Retail, working with agency Halismann Taylor, to address the image of Harvester restaurants. We can all relate to the brief – attempt to shed the Harvester's association with old-fashioned, out-of-date dining. The public relations solution, or at least one of them, was to ban peas from the Harvester menu. The result, a contrived national debate, worked in terms of media coverage and, in the short term at least, increased sales.

In a sense this sums up the need for ambitious creative thinking for services brands, as the question was, 'How do we re-launch our restaurants?' and the answer 'By banning peas'.

5 and 6. Thought leadership and intellectual capital

Surely two of the most overused phrases in the public relations lexicon – but two of the most important when it comes to services public relations. But what do they mean in practice?

In our experience, all industries, sectors and professions are permanently at a crucial stage of their development. The next few years will determine the state of the industry/sector/profession for years to come. Always. Today's crucial issues exercise the minds of industry bodies, politicians and opinion-formers, including senior journalists. The front pages, two-page news analyses and editorial comments of trade publications are largely devoted to these crucial issues. And in all fields, some companies are movers and shakers in these crucial debates. They have a view on whether the big international players are poised to take over, whether the niche specialists will survive and whether the middle tier will be forced out.

Thought leaders are big enough and bold enough to shoot from the hip over the latest Government or Regulator announcement and consultation document. Thought leaders know whether the demographic time-bomb is changing work practices in their industry or affecting the consumer dynamic. They have a view on the impact of technological change, the introduction of the Euro, the breakdown of the traditional family, the blame culture and the rise of litigation.

Sometimes these crucial issues even turn out to be crucial, and sometimes they even determine the shape of the industry/sector/profession for years to come. The de-regulation of the opticians market is a case in point. More often than not, however, the industry/sector/profession enters another crucial phase. Through it all some companies have views on all issues and try to shape their sectors, some have views on certain issues – and many have no clear public views on the issues of the day. The companies that have views receive the most media coverage and attention. They appear dynamic, futuristic and forward-looking. People see them as one of the winners in the future, because they appear to know what it will be. We call them the 'thought leaders'; most people simply see them as leaders.

Intellectual capital is often the same as thought leadership and the two certainly overlap. In our view, however, it's different – and it's particularly important for service companies and certain sections of the service 'industry' in particular (eg, lawyers, management consultants, marketing services and accountants).

For a law firm, differentiating itself from its key competitors in the eyes of its potential clients is particularly difficult. Beyond certain image dimensions – Clifford Chance is 'big and international', Herbert Smith is 'aggressive and dynamic' – there is little between the major law firms in most clients' eyes. Hence the importance of personal recommendation, seminars, conferences and PR.

Law firms still debate endlessly the value of allowing their views to be aired publicly. Will it reveal their hand? Is it fair to their paying clients? The answer, I believe, is that judicious use of their intellectual capital is the only way of differentiating them from the competition on a sustainable basis. What are the implications of divorce? Will the best people want to be non-executive directors in the post-Higgs world? How should corporate behaviour change in a more litigious society? These subjects take law firms to the centre of their clients' world, where they desire to be. Like so many service industries, intellectual capital is really all they have, and they need to use it to define better images and identities.

7. Specialist media relations

Are media relations specialists any more important for services companies than for other companies? Certainly *PR Week*'s Contact Directory league tables tend to indicate that this is the case. Seven of the top 10 hi-tech agencies are either specialists or specialist divisions. BGB & Associates is the largest in leisure/travel and Lansons is the largest in financial services. Only professional services and retail are dominated by 'generalist' agencies.

The importance of media relations specialists stems from the fact that the subject matter is complex (certainly in professional services, technology and financial services) and the journalists tend to work in their sectors for long periods. You have to know what you are talking about and, as important, what the journalists are talking about. The power of specialists is increased as the subject matter for many communication programmes – for reasons discussed earlier – is demonstrating thought leadership and leveraging intellectual capital.

The massive advances in technology have also played a role. The press release is virtually redundant as a tool for reaching national journalists now that hundreds of companies in all fields run professional media relations programmes and many of them have a benchmark 'releases per month' target to meet. Modern technology means that while all of these releases may reach their target in a physical sense, few of them actually get through. And it's becoming the same with e-mail, as journalists' e-mail addresses become 'directoryfied' and thereby very full, all of the time. Bizarrely, the march of technology has left the telephone as the unchallenged king of media contact; you just have to be a specialist to know how to use it.

If you add to that the need to understand journalists' deadlines (Why are you calling me on a Friday afternoon?), pagination (But we don't do product reviews) and news context (So how is your announcement affected by yesterday's Government review and your main competitor's statement?), then you have a mountain to climb as a generalist, or even as a multi-specialist, as modern generalists are known. But then as Chief Executive of a specialist agency I could be accused of bias.

8. Brand association

If you can't think of any other way of communicating innovation, then approach News International and negotiate to sponsor (or create) their 'innovation awards'. It can work too, although the media and publishing world now sees service companies, particularly consultants, lawyers, accountants and software and technology businesses, as cash cows for financing their awards dinners, conferences and seminars. This puts a premium on new events, cleverly designed events and well-targeted events – or equally clever brand associations.

The concept of two brands coming together for mutual benefit is something we'll see more of in years to come. As yet it's mainly a commercial organization and a charity, or a commercial organization and a cultural or sporting event. In future though, I believe that we'll see more 'commercial organization with another commercial organization' brand associations. The rules, as ever, are common sense, but they're all too often forgotten. The appropriateness of choosing a 'partner' is dealt with in Chapter 10, on sponsorship.

9. A sense of mystique

The subtext of much of this chapter thus far is that service companies' offerings are intangible and often complex, and that better, more open communication will lead to a better-defined reputation. But maybe that's not true in all cases. What if familiarity sometimes breeds contempt – or that a sense of mystique is itself sometimes a valuable image attribute?

In the restaurant world, it's certainly true that the more the confidentiality of the kitchen has been breached, the higher the status of chefs and fine dining and gastro pubs have become. But in the City and in the boardroom, mystique appears a common factor in the success of many leading names. Goldman Sachs receives fees running into tens of millions for many of its projects, but you won't find it falling over itself to explain what it does and how it does it. In fact when it tries in its adverts, promising 'unrelenting thinking' and a 'network of excellence', you can't help feeling slightly short-changed. Surely that's not the essence of it? McKinsey remains the problem-solver of choice in many UK boardrooms and plays on its mystique – where rivals like KPMG and PwC bombard all and sundry with high-quality pieces of intellectual capital and thought leadership on a weekly basis.

Is there a lesson in this for other service brands? For some the answer is yes. Mystique will work as the central brand attribute for a few companies in certain fields. Service companies are after all providers of a service, there to serve, even servants. One of the skills, whether you're a lawyer, interior designer, waitress or investment banker, is to define the relationship with your customers on as 'equal' and respectful a basis as possible. If you're the advertising agency that writes to every single marketing director in the UK congratulating them on their appointment, don't be surprised if you have a lower status than the agency that does its talking on the more elevated planes of the conference platform and the *Campaign* thoughtpiece. There's an extent to which we all want the one we can't have – and given that they are living in the intangible world, all service companies need to have it, somewhere, in their armoury.

TO FINISH...

For 95 per cent of brands more open, more thoughtful communication based around the nine core themes mentioned earlier will result in a more effective communication programme and a better reputation. And to finish we've taken those nine themes and produced a checklist of dos and don'ts in the table below.

Theme	Do	Don't
1. Prove the benefits	Prove (in pounds, metres or minutes) that users of the service are better off than those who don't – or prove that there is a definite need in the market.	Expect words and pictures alone to be enough.
2. Happy customers	Insist that happy customers can be found willing to speak to journalists and be photographed.	Accept that it's too difficult.
3. Third party endorsement	Identify, contact and talk to (influence) the key 'independent' commentators in your sector.	Sit back and wait to be independently assessed and evaluated.
4. Creativity	Hold a national debate on whether or not to ban peas.	Announce that you're re-launching your restaurants with a modern menu.
5. Thought leadership	Have clear views on at least some of the key issues affecting your industry/profession during the current, crucial phase.	Wait for the future to unfold before you – and expect to be seen as a leader.
6. Intellectual leadership	Use some of your more interesting views, thoughts and intelligence to help differentiate you from competitors.	Filter all interesting views and insights from your external communication programmes.
7. Specialist media relations	Make sure that whoever represents your business with journalists is a specialist – and understands you and the sector you're in.	Leave the task of talking to journalists to inexperienced people or generalists (warning – they're now called multi-specialists).
8. Association with other brands	Consider whether your brand plus another brand can make three.	Think that money and big brand association in themselves lead to success.
9. Sense of mystique	Sometimes leave something unsaid, something not explained, something not announced. On occasion wait for them to come to you.	

13

Living in an NGO world

Robert Blood

In 30 years a new global political force has emerged almost from nowhere. It rivals parliamentary parties in influence yet is vastly more trusted by voters. It is led by some of the most capable people in reformist politics. It drives media agendas, discomforts governments and humbles multi-billion dollar corporations. Worldwide it has been estimated to employ 19 million people and enjoy an annual income of $1,100 billion.[1]

This is contemporary activism, aka non-governmental organizations or NGOs, pressure groups, not-for-profits, 'civil society'. One has only to intone the casualty list – Shell, Monsanto, McDonald's, Nike, Nestlé, Huntingdon Life Sciences, the World Trade Organization – to remind ourselves that NGOs collectively represent one of the most powerful political forces driving public opinion today.

In most Western democracies activism is the most influential extra-parliamentary movement after the media. While public confidence in business, after a sunnyish period in the mid-1980s, has fallen to new lows thanks to accounting scandals and company pensions anxieties, support for NGOs has never been higher.

Moreover the gap is constantly widening. The divergence in public support for big business versus NGOs during the 1990s is a re-run of the period in the 1970s when the image of multinationals was badly tarnished by the Lockheed and ITT corruption cases. (Then corporations were criticized for trying to influence the actions of foreign governments. Now they are criticized for *not* trying to influence the actions of foreign governments.) The upshot is that NGOs usually top the public's list of most credible institutions, while governments and big business invariably come bottom.

Not to recognize the impact of NGOs in 2003 would be like not accepting the status of trade unions in 1973. Indeed, activism in the UK and the USA effectively occupies the power zone once dominated by trade unions. Then unions saw NGOs, and especially environmental groups, as a threat to their members' jobs. Today they seek alliances with such groups in campaigns as diverse as cheap Third-World contractors in the garment industry, support for the steel industry and the promotion of organic farming.

NGOs thrive in a world where supranational politics is supplanting the self-sufficient state, a change they have been instrumental in bringing about. Kyoto, the Montreal protocol on protecting the ozone layer, CITES for protecting endangered species, and the Cartagena biosafety protocol on biotechnology in food and agriculture were all NGO-inspired treaties. An estimated 44,000 NGOs are active internationally today. In 1978 there were just 9,500; in 1956, a mere 985. [2]

The developing world is experiencing an even bigger NGO explosion. India is said to have some 1 million national NGOs, Brazil 210,000.[3] A Thai politician said last year that his small country was now home to 12,000 pressure groups – and Greenpeace recently established its pan-Asia office there. Not only do large NGO networks impact indigenous policy-making, they are convenient points of entry for rich first-world NGOs. They have been forming policy alliances and financing local campaigns on pet issues such as genetically engineered food. Corporations may have globalized trade, but NGOs are globalizing politics.

One way to measure the enormous power of modern NGOs is to look at the volunteer networks that underpin many of them. In the US it has been estimated that not-for-profit organizations mobilize 20 billion volunteer hours 'worth' a quarter of a trillion dollars a year.[4] Far from all of this effort is deployed in campaigning, but its scale helps to explain why when a corporation or industry gets into a fight with a well-organized, focused activist group, even just a locally formed one, it is the commercial or government interest that often comes off worst.

The biggest NGOs like Greenpeace and Amnesty have become global 'Super brands' like Coca-Cola and Sony, recognized the world over. More significantly, they are competing for, and winning by the bucket load, that most valuable attribute of the healthy corporate brand – trust. NGOs now win a higher level of trust on environmental, human rights and health issues than governments, the media and corporations *combined*.[5]

NGOs have globalized causes. Through their efforts and their worldwide networks – the Internet has been invaluable – issues like oil industry abuses in developing countries and the use of child labour in cocoa plantations can be used to embarrass corporations and investors in rich countries. Even the remotest indigenous tribe can no longer be considered a 'far-away country ... of whom we know nothing' as Neville Chamberlain infamously described Czechoslovakia when justifying Britain's indifference to its fate in 1938.

NGOs already out-smart and out-think corporations and governments in many critical issues: environmental and habitat protection, health impacts of pollution, indigenous peoples' rights, trade with poor countries, etc. They are the quintessential 'experts with attitude'.

Now NGOs are moulding progressive thinking. Their leaders have been instrumental in constructing a new policy agenda for the radical Left, which has embraced the environmental movement as the route to its own revival after two decades of post-Soviet languor. Issues like trade equity, environmental global commons,[6] sustainable development, indigenous peoples' rights and the governance of multinational corporations dominated the debate of the 'anti globalization Left' at the recent European Social Forum (Genoa, November 2002). The political space in which corporations and other policy-makers have to operate is changing and for once, they are not the ones changing it.

QUANGOS AND FANGOS

The clearest evidence that NGOs really do pull the levers of public opinion is the naked imitation by their natural opponents.

Governments started the process by inventing the Quasi NGO or Quango. In the UK the Commission for Racial Equality and the Equal Opportunities Commission are typical Quangos, created in the late 1970s to allow policy development and public influence wholly funded by, but constitutionally detached from, the government of the day (to the extent that Quangos freely attack their funder's policies).

Now the false NGO – perhaps we should call it the Fango – has arrived. The Fango looks like a real NGO – independent, media savvy, campaigning orientation, a grand-sounding name – but unlike an industry association, hides the source of its funding and motivation while promoting policies helpful to its backers. A Fango may be funded by an industry or sometimes just a single company. The Association for Competitive Technology, the Independent Institute, National Taxpayers Union, and Citizens for a Sound Economy were all alleged to be Microsoft-funded policy fronts designed to sway critical opinion during its long-running US anti-trust case.[7]

Meanwhile the established NGOs seem to be polarizing towards three main types: in addition to 'Super brands' already mentioned, like Greenpeace and Amnesty International, there are what might be called the 'Technicians', eg, WWF, Médicins Sans Frontières, Oxfam, and the 'Ideologues', typified by Friends of the Earth (FoE) and PETA (People for the Ethical Treatment of Animals).

Technician groups are distinguished by their outstanding specialist expertise and technical resources. They are respected for effecting positive change, not just talking about it. Ideologues are motivated by an intensely felt (Utopian?) vision of the future. FoE wants a planet in which environmental considerations are paramount. PETA's goal is a worldwide end to the exploitation of animals (at least by humans).

Technician groups, and to some extent the Super brands, tend to be pragmatic. They will undertake collaborations with corporations and governments to progress common objectives. WWF works with multinationals like Unilever to reduce the impact of palm oil plantations on Indonesian rainforests. Greenpeace sits on Tesco committees about GM food.

Ideologues, however, seek surrender. If compromises are made, they are part of a policy ratchet. PETA campaigned aggressively against McDonald's until it agreed to make meat suppliers raise welfare standards for animals (for a long time McDonald's management resisted on the logical grounds that vegans were not exactly their core market). It then went after Burger King and Wendy's (which rapidly gave in) and is now tackling KFC. Yet these restaurant chains know that once they have all conformed, PETA would start the whole round again with even tougher demands.

MICRO-ACTIVISTS

Recently a fourth type of NGO has become significant: the Micro-activist. Micro-activists are the political children of the Internet. Organized in cells or individuals connected intellectually and ideologically rather than physically, the Internet is both their glue and their wherewithal. Web sites of a mainstream and a one-person NGO are not only hard to distinguish nowadays, they cost a fraction of traditional printed brochures and glossy reports. Moreover, the Internet is superb at attracting and mobilizing like-minded people in worldwide campaigning efforts against selected targets.

On issues like GM foods, animal rights and anti-capitalism/anti-globalization, Micro-activists have achieved much of the campaigning effectiveness of mainstream groups without the managerial and organizational trappings. They have activated the kind of politically conscious individuals, especially the young, who would have been repelled by the hierarchies and 'compromises' of donation/foundation grant-hungry NGOs (although Micro-activists share many of the beliefs of the Ideologues). Far from emulating mainstream NGOs, they are embarrassing them with 'in-your-face' tactics and a greater willingness to attack the perceived perpetrators of wrongs, not merely conduct symbolic direct actions.

Above all, Micro-activists have demonstrated the power of the Internet in contemporary activism. Mainstream groups know the Internet is there but seem unable to extract the same value. Greenpeace claims to have signed up some quarter of a million 'cyberactivists' worldwide but as even it admits, to little effect. Their mistake may have been in seeking quantity rather than quality. Micro-activists can be potent even when they number just a handful, provided they are all whole-heartedly committed to winning the issue. Ideologue groups like FoE have recognized this and have been assiduous in drawing functioning Micro-activist networks into their own campaigns.

Micro-activists have attracted the interest of foundations and endowments, in the USA a vital source of income for small not-for-profit organizations. Not only do foundations get a lot of campaigning 'bang for their buck' with Micro-activists, but being numerous and diverse, there are plenty to choose from. Or a new group can simply be started up. The US 'donor adviser' organization, Tides Center, which annually handles around $40 million in foundation grants, reportedly incubates 350-odd projects – sponsored campaigns or single issue groups – of which some 30 were allegedly created at the behest of a donor.[8]

EUROPE VS THE USA

Due to their different political cultures, Europe and the USA have distinct NGO scenes. Because most European countries elect parliaments under proportional representation, minority parties like the Greens can achieve a significant political voice for the environmental movement. In the USA and the UK they must rely on extra-parliamentary activism, although even in the UK the Greens are making progress as the European Parliament, the Scottish Parliament and the Welsh Assembly now all use proportional representation.

The politicization of environmentalism has advanced furthest in Germany. There the Green Party is large, having roots in both the peace/anti-nuclear movement and environmentalism. Similarly, Greenpeace Germany is the biggest national organization in the Greenpeace network, generating around 40 per cent of the NGO's worldwide income. (Greenpeace Netherlands generates a further 20 per cent and even receives state aid via the Dutch Post Office national lottery.)

In countries with strong consensual traditions – especially the Germano-Nordics – NGOs have been formally included in public policy making, especially when friendly social democratic parties are in power.

That said, widespread state ownership and coddling of industrial interests has until now hampered campaigns for serious legislative change. Unlike the USA, where the courts are widely used as an adjunct to public opinion campaigning, European

NGOs can only in a very limited way judicially challenge government and corporate decisions.

It is striking that Amnesty is the only major NGO that is strong in both the USA and Europe. With the possible exception of WWF/World Wildlife Fund, there are no major environmental NGOs that are equally well represented in both regions (not even Greenpeace). This has allowed the European NGOs to take an overtly anti-US position on issues like Kyoto/climate change and genetically engineered food, which has appealed to European public opinion.

Perhaps it is no coincidence that Europeans have come to feel relatively positive about big NGOs. In a recent study by Edelman,[9] Amnesty, WWF and Greenpeace were trusted by 62 to 76 per cent of Europeans, whereas in the USA they never got more than 43 per cent. By contrast, in the USA Microsoft was more trusted than any big NGO, but lagged badly behind them in Europe. (This cannot easily be put down to anti-Americanism. The German chemical company Bayer was less trusted in Europe than either Microsoft or Ford.)

However, on the major global policy issues the big NGOs worldwide have coalesced regardless of location; only tactics and priorities differ. European NGOs have pushed GM food much harder than US ones, but this largely reflects public traction: having had their confidence shattered by BSE and a raft of other food scares, European consumers were much more ready to believe the worst about GM foods than their US counterparts. US NGOs are far from giving up the struggle, however.

IN THE FIRING LINE

Companies and governments with controversial policies or activities are the traditional targets of NGO campaigning. While well-established NGOs are usually seeking to mould government policy in the long term – for example, environmental groups want more pro-Green legislation – their focus is usually on specific goals or policy objectives, chosen for being both realizable and within the reach of public acceptance. Thus in Germany, while the effort to reduce waste, increase recycling and reduce landfill and incineration is continuous, the most recent NGO focus has been for a law mandating manufacturer refunds for returned drinks bottles and cans. Ostensibly this will save cities having to clear up millions of the things left in the streets by drinkers.

In recent years individual corporates have been more heavily targeted, sometimes, in the case of the animal rights movement, with physical aggression and intimidation. NGOs perceive that companies are not only extremely sensitive about adverse publicity but also increasingly keen to show they are the good guys (or at least not the bad guys) on issues like environmental protection and human rights. Firms may be selected because they are the principal offenders, but sometimes they are targeted simply for tactical effect. Such targets seem to fall into four groups: 'Injured Antelopes', 'Tethered Goats', 'Weakest Links' and 'Red Tabs'.

'Injured Antelopes' – eg, Huntingdon Life Sciences, Shell – are firms with damaged reputations from the past and which therefore remain targets of choice for activists who (like lions sensing the weakest animal in the herd) sense their continuing reputational vulnerability.

'Tethered Goats' are firms that are involved in an 'objectionable' industry but do not have the strength to overcome sustained attack. Because of animal testing the pharmaceutical and medical research industry is hated by animal rights campaigners but it is the small contractors – the specialist breeders and animal lab equipment suppliers – who are being driven out of business.

'Weakest Links' are suppliers that are vital to a targeted industry but where the importance of the relationship is not reciprocal. Farmers need someone to ship animals across the Channel, furriers need retailers to sell furs, all firms need financial institutions – but not the reverse. If the business is relatively small but the reputational risk or hassle is great, the supplier becomes vulnerable. Thus ferry companies no longer carry live animals, department stores no longer sell furs and, as several banks, stockbrokers and even the world's largest insurance adviser found to their cost over Huntingdon Life Sciences, financial services institutions have become the target of choice for ideological activists.

Firms whose position enables them to put pressure on the rest of the supply chain are also natural 'Weakest Links'. For this reason retailers are a favourite target of food, health and farm animal welfare groups. Not only are there relatively few of them per country, but if a retailer can be persuaded to take up an issue – after campaigning at their customers (or threatening to) – they know the new policy will ripple through the supply chain, if needs be down to individual farms.

Snipers in World War I were encouraged to try to shoot at senior officers, easily identified by the red tabs on the lapels of their uniforms (a sartorial practice soon abandoned, at least on the front line). Thus 'Red Tabs' are firms that are targeted precisely because they are the biggest or best known. The logic is that their pre-eminent position makes them vulnerable, and if they can be made to succumb, rivals will have to follow suit. Thus Tesco's is targeted by FoE, Exxon by Greenpeace, Starbucks Coffee by the organic/anti-GM food groups and McDonald's by PETA.

THE FUTURE

As NGOs become more influential and the biggest groups wield obvious power and media attention, they are attracting more frequent criticism, from within and without. Many supporters find themselves philosophically at odds with NGOs behaving like capitalists, occupying fancy glass headquarters and paying high salaries to senior staff. That said, with such a variety of NGOs the seriously unhappy can easily find more congenial billets. Although they often collaborate, Friends of the Earth has a distinctly more laidback and less hierarchical culture than Greenpeace. War on Want is more overtly anti-capitalist than Oxfam despite having similar development agendas.

Paradoxically, high profile successes are also threatening the basis of NGOs' original credibility as 'Davids' confronting industry and government 'Goliaths'. Greenpeace is especially fond of this image, which it sustains with photos of protestors (always described as 'volunteers') in rubber dinghies being mowed down by supertankers. But it begins to look a little odd when the public keeps seeing companies buckling before its campaigns.

National news outlets have attacked Greenpeace for posturing and wasting donations on staff perks. And while Greenpeace was widely applauded for campaigning for a ban on CFCs that were destroying the ozone layer, its grandstanding over the deep sea disposal of Shell's Brent Spar oil rig was widely criticized, not least because Greenpeace seriously misled the public about the amount of polluting oil left in the structure. Greenpeace was quick to admit its mistake but too late to stop the damage to its credibility.

Subsequently the media in the UK flagellated itself for broad-casting without editorial or critical comment Greenpeace's own video footage of its rig occupation.

The GM foods issue has spurred even louder accusations of abuse of power. Shocked by the near-collapse of the world's nascent agri-biotech sector, over 3,000 scientists, including 22 Nobel Prize winners,[10] condemned NGO-inspired absolutist opposition to GM crops. High profile refuseniks like the former president of Greenpeace Canada, Patrick Moore, and Bjorn 'Sceptical Environmentalist' Lomborg, and even some US NGOs like the Rockefeller Foundation and Center for Science in the Public Interest, say NGOs are being ideological and irrational. Questions are being raised about how an organization like Greenpeace that boasts strong scientific credentials can have decided it was right, or even possible, to throw away an entire and rapidly evolving field of technological progress.

Greenpeace and other campaign groups see the GM issue as fundamentally about who controls world food production – farmers or big business. Their critics hope that the fruits of biotechnology will expose the 'hypocrisy' of powerful rich country environmentalists in trying to deny a technology essential to the sustainable nourishment of developing countries. The issue has already exposed a serious fault line between European and US policy-makers. It could yet trigger a similar division in the NGO world.

IMPLICATIONS FOR POLICY-MAKERS

NGOs can no longer, for practical let alone democratic reasons, be excluded from policy formulation. Policy-makers must engage with NGOs but must first understand their underlying ideological motivations and factor how policy positions will play against internal politics.

All major corporates, and many small ones in controversial sectors, can expect to receive the attentions of NGOs. Increasingly, campaigns will be personalized and cover a range of sensitive pressure points, from employees and potential graduate entrants to suppliers and investors. Are these stakeholders being engaged before NGO pressure is felt? Will they be supportive or indifferent? Can they be involved in policy development to insulate the organization from unreasonable demands?

NGOs are feared for their power, but where does this power really come from? Size of membership? Income? Public endorsement? Commitment? NGOs vary hugely on these parameters. Policy-makers need to be more sophisticated in analysing the range of forces they appear to be working against.

Many NGOs want to see positive results and are willing to work with corporations and others who share the same goals, and are prepared to negotiate, not merely exchange views. They can contribute valuable expertise and ensure collaborative projects are not only publicly validated but also properly executed. Collaborations also build mutual appreciation and break down ideological rigidity on all sides. Understanding what motivates oppositional NGOs and their strengths and weaknesses can help guide the best choice of partner.

The public are willing to see NGOs become more influential because they appear to counterbalance political and corporate power and prevent policy hegemony. But as they become more obviously powerful, will the public begin to demand 'protection' from abuses (as they did with trade unions in Britain during the 1970s)?

Policy-makers and political institutions have yet to grasp the opportunity to rein in NGO extremism by demanding higher and enforceable standards of transparency and internal democracy. But the more thoughtful NGOs are already acknowledging that poor accountability is their Achilles' heel.

CHECKLIST FOR STARTING YOUR OWN NGO

- Goals decide structure – is your purpose short-term and well-defined (eg, to stop a proposed development) or long-term and broad (eg, to defend the interests of an indigenous people)? Short-term campaigns need lots of effort and resources immediately; long-term campaigns can be built up gradually as awareness and expertise deepen.
- Committees are great for broadening support, networking and helping to raise money but they can bog down campaigns in bureaucracy. Day-to-day decisions should be in the hands of a small executive team, ie the people doing the work.

- Fix a strategy and stick to it. What must happen to make your campaign successful? There is usually one, perhaps two, critical decisions or events that determine the outcome of a well-defined campaign. Are you concentrating your efforts on making sure these go your way?
- Do you need to prove you have wide public support? Are you engaging your most obvious potential supporters (other NGOs like environmental, wildlife groups, the local community)?
- You are probably not alone. An Internet search will quickly reveal other groups and campaigns on similar issues, and often a wealth of off-the-shelf campaigning materials.
- Do you need money to pay for publicity materials, staff? Broad-based long-running campaigns should approach foundations, but to succeed you will have to demonstrate a clear need and unique approach. Short-term campaigns rarely require much cash – physical help is more important – unless legal action is contemplated eg, to appeal planning permissions (seek a sympathetic lawyer who will work for you pro bono). Local businesses directly affected by the issue can be helpful with money or services-in-kind. National NGOs like FoE sometimes will resource important local campaigns if a point of principle is at stake.
- Don't forget the media. The cheapness and accessibility of the Internet can lead campaigners to think conventional media are no longer important, but Web sites can end up preaching to the converted. Short-term campaigns should especially cultivate local media contacts (a single point of contact is best). Campaigns must create their own publicity; reacting to the opposition is not enough. Create stunts, do surveys, mount demos, focus on micro-issues – anything to create new stories that will keep your campaign in the public eye.
- Don't stop fundraising. Many campaigns, especially local ones, depend on local retired people and students because they have plenty of time and energy. But they still need money to pay for materials, telephone calls and computer supplies. You should expect to be seeking money constantly from the public and other sources.

CHECKLIST FOR DEALING WITH AN NGO

- Are you the ultimate target of the NGO campaign or merely a tactical objective? Use the analysis suggested in 'In the firing line' above to find out.

- Study the aims and objectives of the NGO and its allies. How are they differentiated? Are some less radical (more 'reasonable') than others? Perhaps you can work with the latter and develop compromise or cooperative solutions. This will help split the common front and reduce public support for extremist ideas.
- Local campaigners often claim to represent the whole of their community. In fact they probably represent only 10 per cent, but the silent majority may be giving them tacit support for historical/political reasons or simply because they do not like to see a 'done deal' in your favour. Avoid ending up trading insults with your direct opponents. It may be satisfying but you are probably bypassing your most important audience – the majority. How are you going to win them over?
- Are your relationships with the media and the public as good as those of your opponents? If you are only thinking about this now, it may be too late.
- Your employees, suppliers or customers may be targeted with pressure, sometimes even intimidation. Are you doing everything you can to protect them? Are they informed about the issue and are you helping them to help defend you?
- Campaigners, like politicians, use emotional messages and images to convey their opposition. These are highly arousing to the public, grab attention (at least in the short term) and demand a response. Corporates, especially technology-based ones, communicate rationally, relying on facts and what to them are logical arguments. The two styles are incompatible. In the public mind it is easy to end up appearing like you are wriggling and avoiding addressing the real issues. Emotional arguments must be opposed with emotional counter-arguments, not 'facts'.
- If public opinion is the ultimate decision-maker, then trust decides everything. Unfortunately NGOs, by definition, invariably start off being much more trusted. It is hard to reduce public trust in an NGO short of showing they are being deliberately fraudulent, so attracting trust to your own case is essential. Openness, responsiveness, engagement with critics, clear leadership, direct and uncomplicated communication and cooption of trusted institutions eg, doctors in a health issue, farmers in a food issue, are all important.
- Dealing with an NGO campaign can consume huge amounts of management time and distract senior staff from running the business. If the opposition is very hot, it is worth setting up a

special management group with the authority and resources to coordinate the counter-campaign. It should not become the preserve of the Chairperson, although if suitable he or she might be its public face. As in all PR work, time invested in relationship building with media, customers, employees, etc, before issues arise, will pay for itself many times over when there is a crisis.

Notes

1. 'NGOs find success brings problems', Quentin Peel, *Financial Times*, 12 July 2001.
2. Union of International Associations, http://www.uia.org/uias-tats/ytb299.htm.
3. 'Ford Foundation cited in NGOs find success brings problems', Quentin Peel, *Financial Times*, 12 July 2001.
4. 'The Nonprofit Piece of the Global Puzzle', Dr Susan Raymond, Changing Our World, Inc. 15 Oct 2001, http://www.onphilan-thropy.com/op2001-10-15.html.
5. Relationship between NGOs, government, media and corporate sector, Richard Edelman, March 2001, http://www.edelman. com/people_and_perspectives/insights/ngo.ppt.
6. Environmental global commons is the notion that rights to interfere with or consume the environment cannot be 'owned' by individuals, only by the community as a whole, cf. common land in villages. Indeed, the sort of people who expound this idea cite by analogy the disappearance of common land in England through the so-called Enclosure Acts, saying that this disenfranchized peasants in favour of the rich.
7. 'Oracle defends Microsoft spying', BBC News online, 29 June 2000.
8. Activistcash.com, http://activistcash.com/.
9. Relationship between NGOs, government, media and corporate sector, Richard Edelman, March 2001, http://www.edelman.com/people_and_perspectives/insights/ngo.ppt.
10. 'Scientists in support of agricultural biotechnology', petition organized by Professor C S Prakash of Tuskegee Institute, Alabama, http://www.agbioworld.com.

Index

NB: page numbers in *italic* indicate figures and tables